Table of Conter

1 • TAXES

Best remaining tax shelter in America....1
Making the most of your medical deductions....2
Unusual medical deductions....2
Pay your child a tax-deductible allowance....3
Personal deduction for corporate donation....3
Add up what you spend on your daughter's wedding, and use it to reduce your income tax....3
A legal way to deduct your gambling losses....4
Commuting cost loophole....4
Parents supported by more than one child: Who takes deduction?....4
Divorce and the IRS....4
Deduct the cost of your hobby as a business expense, even if you never show a profit....5
How to deduct a family vacation as business expenses. (Ingenious possibilities your accountant never showed you.)....6
You're always safe taking the standard deduction, right? Wrong....6
Negligence or tax fraud?....6
Avoiding a tax audit: What IRS computers are looking for on your return—and how to put them off the scent....7
Risk of tax audit depends on how you show what you do for a living. Is your occupation on the IRS hit list?....7
What you don't have to tell an IRS auditor—and how to prevent a "fishing" expedition through your records....8
Why the most dangerous tax audit comes right after you die. Yet...honestly...you can actually fight back from the grave. (And your chances are better dead than alive!)....9
IRS envelope labels—what the numbers really mean....9
How competent/incompetent is your accountant? Check him out...secretly....9
How to cut your state taxes....10

2 • BANKS & CREDIT CARDS

How banks play tricks with interest rates....11
What banks don't tell you....11
Safeguards for safe-deposit boxes...and the little-known vulnerability that makes you a sitting duck....12
When the bank can't bounce a check....12
Checks marked "Payment in Full"....12
How to deposit an unsigned check....12
Credit cards: Beating the system....12
Stretching due dates on bills....13
Twelve ways to avoid being ripped off by your bank....13
The 20 safest banks in the U.S.—and the lemons, which spend their time lending to third-world deadbeats....14

3 • HEALTH

How and where to get the best deals when joining a health club—you can save plenty. And how can you spot a club or sports center that's best avoided?....15
Health club routines that can ruin your back and knees....15
Medicines that can hurt you when you exercise....16
Exercises you can do when stuck in traffic....16
Working off a big meal is easier than you think....16
Vitamin E warning....16
The two famous cold remedies that, taken together, can give you ulcers....16
Pros and cons of vasectomy....16
Relieve a headache without drugs....17
When painkillers cause more pain....17
Sexual side effects of widely used medicines....17
Use sleeping pills without becoming addicted....18
Facts and fallacies about dental care...and the newest technologies already available....18
Why some patients are given favored status in hospitals...almost preferred treatment. This little known information could save your life....19
How to learn about medical discoveries before your doctor....20
Doc-talk: How to translate medical jargon on a patient's hospital chart....20
Questions to ask a surgeon....21
How to get fast emergency medical care....21
Alcohol without hangovers....22
How and when blood pressure can fool you...and drinking alcohol without hangovers....22
Collecting more on your company health policy....22
How to evaluate a nursing home—and the tip-offs that will indicate a rip-off (or worse)....23
Nonstick pan alert....23
Alternative medicine: An Asian cure for the common cold that's amazing the U.S. medical profession....23

9 • REAL ESTATE

10 • ESTATE PLANNING

11 • GETTING YOUR MONEY'S WORTH

12 • CAREER SKILLS

13 • HEALTHY SEX SECRETS

14 • EASY WAYS TO DO HARD THINGS

Taxes

The Best Tax Shelter of Them All

If you own your business, you can take advantage of certain tax strategies to substantially improve your cash flow *and* the quality of your life.

For example, you can have your corporation start a medical reimbursement plan for employees. *Rationale:* The only medical expenses you can deduct on your *personal* tax return are those that exceed 7.5% of adjusted gross income (AGI). So if your AGI is $40,000 and you have medical expenses of $1,000, you're $1,000 out-of-pocket—with no tax benefit whatsoever. But if your company reimburses you, it *can* deduct the $1,000. *Net cash outlay:* $660 if the company is in the 34% tax bracket.

This strategy works only if the plan applies equally to all employees. If it is limited to top officers, they will be taxed as though the reimbursements were salary income. *Caution:* In the case of shareholders, dividend treatment may result. But even that isn't necessarily terrible. You're still better off paying $660 in taxes than $1,000 in medical bills.

The way you take money out of your company makes a difference in your taxes. Dividends are taxed twice—once to your company (because they aren't deductible) and once to you. Salaries are taxed only once. Obviously, the more of your total compensation you take in salary, the better.

There's a limit, though—your salary must be "reasonable." *Guidelines:* Your education, knowledge, expertise...and what top executives in similar companies make. If it appears to the IRS that the reason for the compensation is your ownership interest, it's probably a dividend. If, on the other hand, the reason appears to be the blood, sweat, and tears you put into the company, it's probably salary.

S corporations are a way around the whole salary versus dividends problem. An S corporation pays no taxes itself. Instead, the owners pay taxes on their proportionate share of the company's income. For tax purposes, this is really equivalent to receiving all salary and no dividends. *Drawback:* You have to pay the tax on your share of income *whether or not* you take money out of the company. If your company has loan covenants that *restrict* payment to owners (as many small businesses do), you could have trouble coming up with the cash for taxes.

Perks are another way to use your business to improve your standard of living, and they are nontaxable if you can show they are necessary to your business. That can be tricky. For company cars, you must charge employees fair rental value for any personal use of the car. But the amount you charge can be less than what Hertz charges.

Of course, if a perk fails the necessity test, you can still take a deduction (to the extent your unreimbursed business expenses, together with other miscellaneous itemized deductions, exceed 2% of AGI) for whatever part of the expense is attributable to business. *Example:* Membership dues for a club at which you do a lot of business entertaining. Be sure you have good documentation for any such claims.

Home offices have been attracting attention from the IRS lately. If the home office is for your convenience rather than the company's, and if you have somewhere else to work, you won't be allowed a deduction. *Exception:* If you have a sideline business that produces additional income—such as consulting—and use your home office as either a principal place of business or a place to meet with clients, your deductions for home-office expenses will be allowed.

Other areas in which tax laws play favorites with entrepreneurs:

- Charitable donations. Give stock you hold in your company to charity, then have your company buy it back. You get a deduction for the full market value of the stock—with no personal cash outlay—and the charity gets cash.
- Retirement plans. As a self-employed individual, you can open a Keogh Plan.

Source: Jack Salomon, partner in charge of state tax services at KPMG Peat Marwick, Park Ave. Plaza, 55 E. 52 St., New York 10055.

10 9 8 7 6 5 4 3 2

Printed in the United States of America

Making the Most of Your Medical Deductions

Although medical expenses are deductible only to the extent that, in total, they exceed 7.5% of adjusted gross income, the IRS and court decisions have expanded the definition of medical costs that can be deducted from personal income taxes. Plan ahead to take advantage of as many medical expenses as possible.

Medical deductions can be taken for the costs of diagnosis, the treatment or prevention of a disease, or for affecting any structure or function of the body. *Limitation:* Treatment must be specific and not just for general health improvement.

Example: The IRS successfully denied taxpayers deductions for the cost of weight-control and stop-smoking classes that were designed to improve general health, not to treat a specific ailment or disease. On the other hand, a person with a health problem specifically related to being overweight, such as high blood pressure, might be allowed the deduction.

If an employer tells an overweight employee to lose weight or leave, and the boss has previously enforced such a rule, the plump employee can deduct the cost of a weight-loss program, because money a taxpayer spends to help keep his/her job is deductible. The IRS says it will allow a deduction if two physicians prescribe a weight-reduction program for the treatment of hypertension, obesity, or hearing problems. The same could go for a person whose doctor certifies that a stop to cigarette smoking is necessary for a specific medical reason (such as emphysema).

The same logic applies to home improvements. The cost of a swimming pool would be deductible if it is specifically necessary for a person who has polio, as would the cost of an elevator for a heart patient.

Caution: Only the actual cost (over the increase in value to the property) is deductible. The IRS makes taxpayers subtract from the cost of an improvement the amount that the feature adds to the value of the residence.

Example: If a swimming pool costs $10,000 but adds $4,000 to the value of the property, only $6,000 would be tax deductible. To determine the value, have the property appraised before and after the improvement. (The appraisal fee is tax deductible as a miscellaneous itemized deduction to the extent allowed by the Tax Reform Act of 1986.)

Medical or business? Because medical costs are deductible only after they exceed 7.5% of a taxpayer's adjusted gross income, it is tempting to declare them as business expenses. *Trap:* The IRS rarely allows those business deductions. But there is a sizable gray area. A professional singer was once not allowed to deduct the cost of throat treatments as a business expense, but an IRS agent did allow a deduction for a dancer who found it necessary to her career to have silicone breast implants.

Medically unproven treatment is generally deductible, since the IRS has taken the position that it cannot make judgments in the medical field. *Example:* Laetrile treatments are deductible if the taxpayer receives them legally. Disallowed: A deduction for the cost of a food processor for a special diet consisting of vegetables. Or a special vitamin-enriched diet, even though the taxpayer is diabetic.

Deductions for medical expenses of married children are sometimes possible, provided you contributed more than half of the child's support. *How it works:* The daughter of a highly paid executive ran up medical bills of more than $5,000. She married later that year and filed a joint return with her husband. Nevertheless, her father was allowed to deduct the cost of treatment on his return for the year, even though the daughter didn't qualify as a dependent.

Education: The IRS draws a hard line on deductibility of special schooling for children with medical problems. Not deductible: The cost of attending a school with smaller classes, even for a child with hearing or sight problems. To be eligible to make such a claim, the school would have to offer special programs for children with specific disabilities. *Approved by the IRS:* A deduction for the full cost of sending a child to a boarding school equipped to handle deaf children with emotional problems. Denied by the IRS: A deduction for extra costs, including travel, that was claimed by a parent who sent his deaf child to a distant public school that was better equipped than the local public school to handle such students.

Other deductible costs: Birth-control pills and other prescription drugs, vasectomies, legal abortions.

No longer deductible: Unnecessary cosmetic surgery.

Source: Sidney Kess, attorney & CPA, 630 Fifth Ave., New York 10111.

Unusual Medical Deductions

Payments have been held to be deductible when made to:

- An untrained companion hired to look after an invalid's needs.

•An acupuncturist, even though the state medical association did not recognize acupuncture as a form of medicine.

•A Christian Science practitioner, even though the payer wasn't seeking medical help.

•Social Security taxes on the wages paid to a private nurse.

In addition, deductions have been allowed for the cost of:

•Whiskey prescribed by a physician to relieve pain.

•A wig prescribed by a psychiatrist for a patient upset by hair loss.

•Extra costs for salt-free or other special food prescribed by a doctor.

•A stereo for a person confined to the house by multiple sclerosis.

•Hand controls for the care of a handicapped person.

•A guide dog for a blind person.

•A car telephone for a person who may require instantaneous medical help.

•Transportation to and from an Alcoholics Anonymous center.

•Lip-reading instructions for a person who is hard of hearing.

•The extra cost of braille editions of books for a blind person.

•A reader to assist a blind businessperson at the job.

•Insurance on contact lenses for a person who requires them.

•Extra electricity costs for medically necessary equipment, such as a whirlpool or central air conditioning.

•Travel expenses made necessary by illness. *Example:* The fare to the Mayo Clinic. *Also deductible:* Travel expenses for a nurse to accompany the patient or even for a spouse who performs medical services. *Doubtful:* The cost of living in or moving to a more healthful climate.

•The portion of a housekeeper's salary that goes toward the medical care of a sick resident.

Paying Your Child a Tax-Deductible Allowance

Paying your children to work in your business is a good way of providing tax-deductible allowances. A child with no other income can earn up to $3,800 tax-free (indexed for inflation).

Caution: Keep very good records of the type of work they do and the hours they put in. The mere fact that you pay wages to your children won't trigger an audit. Their pay is lumped in with wages of other employees on your return. But if you are audited for some other reason, the IRS is likely to question this expense. Be prepared to show that the pay was reasonable.

Personal Deduction for Corporate Donation

There is a way for owners of closely held companies to use *company funds* to get a charitable deduction on their *personal* income tax returns. The owner gives the charity stock in his/her company. Subsequently, the company redeems the stock from the charity. *Advantage:* A 100% owner would not give up any ownership interest in the company, since his interest in the company after the charity is redeemed would still be 100%. *How a bailout works:* The owner makes an *informal* agreement with the charity to offer the stock for redemption shortly after the charity receives it. The owner gives the stock to the charity. He takes a deduction on his personal return for the fair market value of the stock. A week or so later, the company redeems the stock from the charity. If the transaction is handled properly, the stock's redemption will not be taxed as a dividend to the owner. *Caution:* The agreement with the charity must be *informal.* The charity must not be under a binding obligation to let the company redeem the stock. It must have the legal right to retain the stock or to sell it to an outsider. *Tax rule:* Normally, if a 100% shareholder in a closely held company has some of his stock redeemed, income from the redemption will be taxed as a dividend. But the IRS has agreed that a redemption will not be considered a dividend if it is handled by an *informal,* prearranged plan with a charity. Such a transaction *must* be structured properly to ensure the desired tax results. Check with your accountant or attorney.

Source: Tom C. Kline, CPA, 330 W. 58 St., New York.

Wedding Gift from IRS

A parent who provides over half of a child's support can claim a dependency exemption if the child is under 19 or a full-time student ($2,450 indexed for inflation). The cost of a child's wedding is considered support. So even if the child lives with a spouse after marriage, the wedding may push the parent's support cost over the 50% mark and entitle the parent to the exemption.

Drawback: The newlyweds cannot file a joint return for the year, nor can the child claim the personal exemption for himself.

Source: *Revenue Ruling* 76–184.

Deductible Gambling Losses

With luck, you might win big. *Trap:* Winnings are taxable, and winnings of over $600 are reported to the IRS.

The tax can be cut by netting the gain against gambling losses, but few people document their losings. *Result:* A person who scores a big win may wind up paying tax on the gain without getting any benefit from his/her losses. He may wind up paying extra tax even if he *lost more than he won* over the entire year.

Better way: Keep tabs on your gains *and* losses. The IRS recommends wagering tickets, canceled checks, credit records, bank withdrawal statements, and credit receipts as proof. An accurate *diary* is also recommended.

Bottom line: The result of *all kinds* of gambling is netted at year-end to determine the size of any gain. So if you are planning to be lucky at all this year, keep records for the *entire* year.

Source: Dr. Robert S. Holzman, professor emeritus of taxation at New York University, and the author of *Estate Planning: The New Golden Opportunities*. Boardroom Books, Springfield, NJ 07081.

Commuting Cost Loophole

A home office can generate extra tax savings. Use it to convert nondeductible commuting costs into deductible travel expenses.

Key: While the cost of commuting between home and work is normally not deductible, the cost of traveling between different job sites is a deductible travel expense. And a home office can have the effect of converting your home into a job site.

That's what the tax court ruled in the case of an insurance salesman who deducted all his auto-travel expenses. The IRS allowed the salesman's deduction for trips from one client to another, but disallowed his deduction for daily travel from home to his sales area. The home office saved the day. The tax court found that the salesman's home was a place of business, so all his travel costs were deductible.

Carl F. Worden, TC Memo 1981-366.

Parents Supported by More Than One Child: Who Takes Deduction?

When brothers and sisters support a parent, plan things so that one of them can deduct the parent's medical expenses: *Here's how:*

First step: File a multiple-support declaration (Form 2120). Where several people contribute, this form designates the one who can take the exemption. If they pay at least 10% each, but nobody gives as much as half, any *one* of them may take the exemption *if* the others agree.

Second step: The one claiming the exemption should pay doctor bills directly and make clear (on the check) that his contribution is *earmarked* for medical expenses. Then he can deduct the parent's medical expenses on his tax return. *Remember:* Medical expenses can be deducted only for yourself, your spouse, and your dependents. You can't take a deduction for medical expenses paid for somebody else unless you can *properly* claim the person as a dependent.

Divorce and the IRS

Basic tax principles to keep in mind:

Alimony payments of cash, checks, and money orders payable on demand are tax deductible by the spouse who pays them and taxable income to the spouse who receives them. No other payments are deductible. *Exception:* Either spouse can claim medical expenses for the children, subject to the 7.5% floor on the deductibility of medical expenses.

Child support, lump-sum payments, wife's legal fees, premiums on life insurance policies owned by the husband—all these are *not deductible* by the spouse paying them. And they need not be reported as income by the spouse who receives the payments.

In the still common case among executives where the husband has a large taxable income and the nonworking wife has little or none, it probably makes sense to make all the payments as *alimony* rather than as something else. The result is to shift income from the husband's high bracket to the wife's lower bracket. It's essential to prepare carefully several alternative plans, varying the mix among alimony and other types of payments, and figuring the available income from each after taxes. *Keep in mind that:*

The dependency exemption for children of divorced or separated parents will be given to the custodial parent unless he/she agrees in writing to waive the exemption. Thus, the father can probably claim them even if they live with the mother. Of course, only one parent can claim them. (If the husband's tax return comes up for audit, the IRS may track down the wife's return, even if she lives in another IRS district.)

A parent who has a child living with him/her may be able to file as a (tax-favored) *head of household* by claiming that child as a dependent.

Conceivably, *both* parents might have *head-of-household* status. This could happen if the younger children stayed with Mother, but an older child—away at college full-time—stayed with Father when home on vacation.

Child support normally stops when the children become independent. *Alimony* often goes on until the wife remarries.

If it's agreed that the husband will pay for the wife's divorce lawyer, estimate the fee and add this amount to the alimony that has been negotiated. Then get a deduction for the amount. But don't forget that it's income to the wife in this case.

How to Deduct Your Hobby

For your own bottom line, it can make a huge difference whether you operate a hobby as a *hobby* or as a *sideline business.* As a hobbyist, your tax deductions are pretty much limited to the amount of income the activity generates. But if you run the hobby as a business, your expenses are deductible even if they *exceed* business income.

Problem: The distinction between a hobby and a business is very fine. When you deduct losses from a business that the IRS could label as a hobby, you must be able to prove that you intended to make a profit.

As far as the IRS is concerned, a *business* is an activity engaged in for *profit.* There's no law, however, that says you must actually *make* a profit. The only rule is that you must *intend* to make a profit.

Presumption of law that aids taxpayers: If you show a profit in three of any five consecutive years (two out of seven for breeding, showing, training, or racing horses), it is presumed that you are engaged in an activity for profit. Although the IRS can challenge the presumption, normally it will not.

You can elect to delay any IRS determination until the first five years are up by filing Form 5213. But in making this election, you sign a waiver of the three-year statute of limitations on sideline business items for the tax years involved.

Profit Motive

If you don't meet the presumption, the IRS may challenge your deductions as *hobby losses.* It will be necessary for you to prove your good intentions. Here's a checklist of things you should be prepared to show the IRS if your business losses are challenged:

- You operate in a businesslike manner. Keep accurate books and records.
- You instituted new operating procedures to correct past business practices that resulted in losses.
- You act professionally. Show that you hired or consulted with recognized experts in the field, and that you followed their advice.
- You made a serious effort. Show that you hired qualified people to run your day-to-day operation. No rule says *you* must devote 40 hours a week to your sideline business.
- There is a profit potential. Even if your business continually produces losses, you can still prove a profit motive by showing that assets you have acquired are expected to appreciate.
- You have had past successes. It may help establish a profit motive if you show that in the past you were successfully involved in your current activity.

Doing Business

The IRS will look for tangible indications that you have really embarked on a business enterprise. *Suggestions:*

- Register your business name by filing a *"doing business as"* statement with your local county clerk.
- Use business cards and stationery.
- Take out a company listing in the Yellow Pages.
- Keep a log of the business contacts you've seen during the year.
- Advertise in local papers.
- Send promotional mailings to prospective customers.
- Set up a business bank account.
- Get a business telephone.
- Buy a postage meter and a copying machine.
- Hire at least some part-time help.

Tougher Questions

Although it's unfair, the IRS will argue that, since you had other sources of income and could afford to lose money, you could not have had a profit motive. *Your defense:* Nobody expects to lose forever. Even with your tax deductions, you would have been better off had you done nothing and never started the venture in the first place.

Suppose your business occasionally generates small amounts of income. You could prove to the IRS a profit motive if you can also show an opportunity to earn a substantial *ultimate* profit in a highly speculative business.

If the IRS can show that you derive personal pleasure from your business, it will count this against you. Businesses that involve horse racing, farming, car racing, and antiques are particularly vulnerable to this kind of attack. *Don't let the IRS bulldoze you.* The courts have consistently held that enjoying what you do is not, by itself, proof that you lack a profit motive.

Source: Randy Bruce Blaustein, Esq., a former IRS agent now with Blaustein, Greenberg & Co., 155 E. 31 St., New York 10016. He is the author of *How to Do Business with the IRS,* Prentice-Hall, Englewood Cliffs, NJ 07632, and *Tax Shelters: Shrewd Insights,* Boardroom Books, Springfield, NJ 07081.

Deducting Vacation Costs As Business Expenses

Combining a tax-deductible business trip with a short vacation, perhaps with a spouse and family, can be quite attractive. It is important to keep expense categories straight, since different tests apply for deductibility.

You can deduct the cost of traveling in the US for business purposes. But you must be able to show that the primary purpose of the trip was business. This does not mean that you cannot combine business with pleasure, only that the primary purpose be business. *Best way to satisfy the IRS:* Prove that more than half of your time at the destination was spent on business.

The all-or-nothing test for travel: Your transportation expenses (airfare, cabs, etc.) are either fully deductible or they cannot be deducted at all. On the other hand, business meal and entertainment expenses at your destination are 50% deductible. Expenses qualify as business meals or business entertainment only if business is actually discussed.

You can't deduct your spouse's expenses. It is not enough for the IRS that a spouse's presence is a big help to you. *Only your expenses at the meeting site are deductible,* but you are not limited to half of the total costs there. You can still deduct the full amount of what it would cost you to attend alone at the single-room hotel rate, for instance. You can deduct the full cost of services where your spouse's presence does not boost the charge, say, for the taxi from the airport. If you drive to the meeting site, you can deduct almost the full transportation cost. If you fly or take the train, only *your* ticket is deductible.

For business-vacation combinations of seven days or less to spots outside the US, the regular rules on business travel, explained above, apply. But if you are gone for more than seven days and you spend more than 25% of your total time vacationing, you lose a deduction for the portion of your transportation costs that is equal to the number of nonbusiness days divided by the total number of days outside the US.

The rules are tighter for conventions outside the North American area. No costs can be deducted for such a business meeting unless the IRS can be convinced that the selection of the meeting site is reasonable. (In practice, it is probably better to be able to prove that it is more reasonable to hold the convention at the foreign site than in the US.)

No deduction is permitted for travel to investment seminars or investment conventions.

Ship travel can be an asset on a combined business-vacation trip. *Reason:* Days spent in transit count as business days in the allocation formula. *Example:* A two-day business meeting in Paris is followed by a two-week European vacation. If you fly (one day each way), only 22% is deductible (two business days plus two days of travel out of a total of 18 days away). But if you sail (five days each way), 46% is deductible (two business days plus 10 days of travel out of a total of 26 days away).

Good records are needed to justify your deductions. *Required:* Keep a diary in which you record expenses and their business purpose. You must also keep receipts for expenses of $25 or more. The diary alone is sufficient proof for smaller amounts.

Source: Edward Mendlowitz, partner, Mendlowitz Weitsen, CPAs, 2 Pennsylvania Plaza, New York 10121, and the author of *Successful Tax Planning,* Boardroom Books, Springfield, NJ 07081.

You're Always Safe Taking the Standard Deduction, Right? Wrong

Self-employed people are likely to have their returns audited if they take the standard deduction instead of itemizing personal nonbusiness deductions, especially if their business shows a high gross and a low net. The IRS will suspect that personal expenses have been charged to the business.

Negligence or Tax Fraud?

Failure to report income deposited in a bank could be considered careless. That is punishable by a 5% negligence penalty. But when the omitted income represented deposits made in a bank in a different state, one court regarded the omission as a fraudulent, willful attempt to conceal income.

Source: *Candella et al. vs. United States,* USDC, E. Dist. WI.

Minimizing Chances of Tax Audit

To be perfectly candid, there is no way of being sure that your federal income tax return won't be audited. Even overpaying won't protect you from IRS scrutiny. Some returns are pulled out by random selection. Others are chosen by IRS computers, which analyze returns to score the likelihood of collecting further. Computers select a return for audit if medical expenses, contributions, property taxes, etc., represent an unusually high percentage of the taxpayer's income (according to nationwide experience). Returns also invite scrutiny when figures do not agree with other information received by the IRS. (A corporation reports on form 1099 that it paid $2,000 in dividends to a taxpayer, but that taxpayer reports only $1,000.) And returns may be audited by reason of tips provided by tax informants.

But your chances of being audited can be reduced greatly by following these suggestions:

1. Answer *all* questions on the tax return form.

2. Complete all schedules that are required. Use the words *None* or *Not applicable* where appropriate.

3. Include full documentation of items that are certain to be questioned, such as large casualty losses or large moving expenses. If the IRS asks for unsupplied substantiation, expect this request to come up with additional questions in other areas of the return at the same time.

4. Send tax returns and other documents to the right office at the right time so that correspondence and personal contact aren't necessary. Once begun, such correspondence or contact is often difficult to end, for one thing leads to another.

5. Don't deduct a type of item that had been disallowed on a previous tax return. The IRS may remember this and look for a repeat.

6. Don't use a tax preparer of dubious character. If the IRS, through its investigators, finds a preparer who is grossly incompetent *or worse,* the names of all his clients will be obtained. All of them, however innocent, will have their tax returns checked by experts in this sort of thing.

7. Be certain that the return has the right signatures and identifying numbers. If it is a corporate return, the title of the signer should be one of the officers *authorized by law* to sign.

Many audits are triggered by:

•*Information returns from banks, investments, or employers* that show payments (dividends, interest, salaries, or fees) that differ from those reported.

•*Unusually large deductions*. The computer flags deductions that are much larger than the *average* amount taken by most taxpayers in the same income group. *Suggestions:* Provide some details on extra-large deductions. Big casualty loss? Describe the hurricane or flood, maybe even enclose a newspaper clipping. Give dates and details of a long illness or a serious accident that produced large medical deductions.

•*Unbelievable numbers.* Such as claiming that you held real estate or IBM stock for 25 years and sold it at a loss. Or large deductions and losses that leave no money to live on. Business expenses that are out of line with the amount of gross income or the nature of the business. Or mortgage interest and property tax deductions that are unusual in the area in which you live.

•*Large round numbers.* Raises questions as to whether you just picked an exaggerated number out of the air without supporting documentation.

•*Office at home*. Getting closer scrutiny because the rules are now much tougher.

Important: If the IRS strikes gold in auditing a return, it will often go after other members of the family, or partners, employees, and other stockholders in the same S corporation.

IRS Hit List

Doctors and *dentists* are high-priority targets. *Items IRS agents look for:* Dubious promotional expenses. If the same four people take turns having lunch together once a week and take turns picking up the tab, a close examination of diaries and logbooks will show this. Agents also take a close look at limited-partnership investments, seeking signs of abusive tax shelters. And they take a dim view of fellowship exclusions claimed by medical residents.

Other target occupations:

•*Salespeople:* Salespeople who work outside and auto salespeople are particular favorites. Agents look for, and often find, poorly documented travel expenses and padded promotional figures.

•*Airline pilots:* High incomes, a propensity to invest in questionable tax shelters, and commuting expenses claimed as business travel make them inviting prospects.

•*Flight attendants:* Travel expenses are usually a high percentage of their total income and often aren't well documented. Some persist in trying to deduct panty hose, permanents, cosmetics, and similar items that the courts have repeatedly ruled are personal rather than business expenses.

•*Executives:* As a group they are not usually singled out. But if the return includes Form 2106, showing a sizable sum for unreimbursed employee business expenses, an audit *is* more likely. Of course, anyone whose income is over $50,000 a year is a high-priority target just because of the sums involved.

• *Teachers and college professors:* Agents pounce on returns claiming office-at-home deductions. They are also wary of educational expense deductions because they may turn out to be vacations in disguise.

• *Clergymen:* Bona fide priests, ministers, and rabbis aren't considered a problem group. But if W-2s show income from nonchurch employers, the IRS will be on the alert for mail-order-ministry scams.

• *Waitresses, cabdrivers, etc.* Anyone in an occupation where tips are a significant factor is likely to get a closer look from the IRS nowadays.

Many people, aware their profession subjects them to IRS scrutiny, use nebulous terms to describe what they do. Professionals in private practice may list themselves as simply "self-employed." Waitresses become "culinary employees," pilots list themselves as "transportation executives." But there's a fine line here. Truly deceptive descriptions could trigger penalties. And if the return *is* chosen for audit, an unorthodox job title for a mundane profession could persuade the agent that you have something to hide. Then he'll dig all the deeper.

Source: Ralph J. Pribble, a former IRS field agent, president of Tax Corporation of California, 5420 Geary Blvd., San Francisco 94121.

How to Handle an IRS Auditor

The more time you put between initial contact by the IRS and your first appointment with the auditor, the better off you'll be. *Reason:* Revenue agents are under considerable pressure to close their quota of cases within a set period of time. The longer your case has been in the agent's inventory, the more likely he is to rush through the audit—to your advantage.

How to buy time: Telephone to ask for an extension. Do this the day before your appointment, not the day you get the appointment letter. By then, the agent will be booked up with other cases for six weeks or so.

If you're persistent, and you have legitimate reasons for extensions, you can generally postpone the audit for up to six months. *Caution:* Don't ask for a postponement without a good excuse. Stalling can backfire by antagonizing the agent.

Presenting Your Case

Prepare meticulously for the audit. Gather all your receipts for the deductions the IRS has questioned. List each, in detail, on a sheet of paper. Also, meticulously reconstruct cash expenditures for which you don't have receipts. Explain exactly how and when you made those expenditures.

By presenting your case in factual detail, you establish your credibility. And *credibility is everything* at an audit. It will be easier for the auditor to allow nondocumented items if you can show him that you kept some receipts, that you made an effort to comply with IRS rules and regulations, and that you've reconstructed, as best you could, your cash outlays.

T&E Audits

Travel and entertainment is the most commonly audited deduction. *Your goal:* To limit the items the agent examines by persuading him to do a *test check* of your expenses. Let the auditor choose a three-month period for detailed examination. Or talk him into limiting the audit to items over, say, $100. Make sure you can document all items in the test-check period or in the amount. Keep a T&E expense diary. *Double benefit:* A test check cuts down your work in assembling back data, and it prevents the agent from rummaging through *all* your travel and entertainment expenses.

Keep Talking

Don't expect to walk out of an audit not owing a dime. Your objective is to strike the best possible deal. *To get an auditor to see things your way:* Keep harping on the items he says must be adjusted. Keep talking. Don't give up until he reduces the adjustment. Even the most hard-nosed agent will ultimately concede some proposed adjustments if you're stubborn enough. But you must be prepared to give a little, too—to concede items you're weak on, to bargain. Keep in mind that the agent's goal is to close the case and move on to his next audit.

Special Problems

Business audits: If your business is being audited, have it done at your accountant's office, *not* at your home or your place of business. You don't want the auditor to see your standard of living or run the risk that an employee will say something to the auditor that could hurt you.

Unreported income: A question generally asked at IRS audits is, *Have you reported all your income?* Never answer this or other potentially embarrassing questions with a lie. *Deliberately failing to report all your income is a crime. So is lying to an IRS employee.* To avoid incriminating yourself, deflect the question with, *Why do you want to know that?* or *I'll get back to you on that later.* The question may not come up again. Another way to avoid answering this question is to not show up for the audit. Then the deductions you've been asked to prove will automatically be disallowed. But you can *appeal* the agent's disallowance at the appeals level of the IRS. At the appeals level, you're generally not asked whether you've reported all your income.

Special agents: Their job is to develop evidence for *criminal* tax cases. If they show up at your door, don't answer *any* of their questions, even seemingly innocuous ones. Tell them to talk with your lawyer. Then retain a lawyer who is knowledgeable in criminal tax matters. *Best:* A former assistant US attorney.

Source: Randy Bruce Blaustein, Esq., a former IRS agent, now with Blaustein, Greenberg & Co., 155 E. 31 St., New York 10016. Mr. Blaustein is the author of *How to Do Business with the IRS,* Prentice-Hall, Englewood Cliffs, NJ 07632, and *Tax Shelters: Shrewd Insights,* Boardroom Books, Springfield, NJ 07081.

Scariest Tax Audit Is the One Right After You Die

It is standard operating procedure for the IRS to examine the federal income tax returns of a decedent for the three years prior to his/her death.

Unless clear and well-documented work papers can be shown and explained to the IRS by a knowledgeable person familiar with the facts, there are apt to be disallowances because of lack of substantiation.

Can your returns be explained satisfactorily by someone else when you are not available?

Information as to where records are located should not be in the will. Instead, include it in a separate communication to the executor in advance, or leave it among personal possessions.

Source: *Estate Planning: The New Golden Opportunities,* by Robert S. Holzman, Boardroom Books, Springfield, NJ 07081.

IRS Envelope Labels—What The Numbers Really Mean

Here's the scoop on the numbers and symbols on the peel-off label the IRS sends with your tax package.

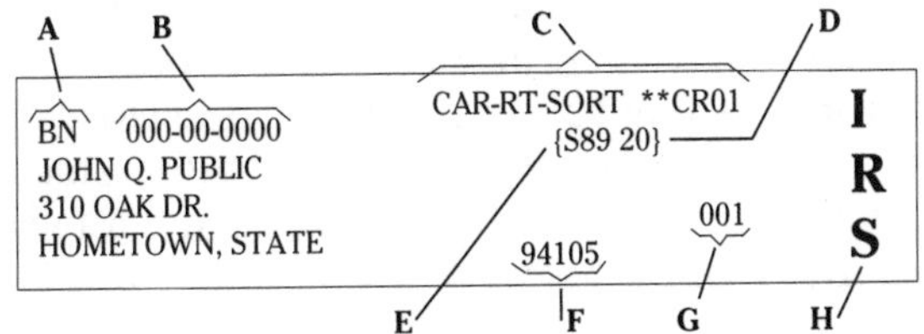

A. Two-letter "alpha code" that is computer shorthand for your name.

B. Your Social Security number. By entering the two-letter code and your Social Security number, the IRS can identify the correct account. The data-entry clerk doesn't have to type your full name and address into the computer.

C. Postal Service home-delivery route.

D. Type of package mailed to the taxpayer—1040, 1040A, etc.

E. IRS service center where you filed your return last year—in this case, Fresno, CA. (S89 is the Ogden service center, Kansas City is S09, etc.)

F. Your postal ZIP code.

G. The IRS's presort mail for the US Postal Service.

H. Certain labels, to help with mail distribution, have either PP, SS, or PL directly under the "S" in IRS. *These letters indicate:*

- PP—Package (first label in a package).
- SS—Sack (first label in a sack).
- PL—Pallet (first label in a pallet).

Source: George S. Alberts, former director of the Albany and Brooklyn IRS district offices.

How Competent/Incompetent Is Your Accountant? Check Him Out...Secretly

Accountants, like lawyers, are licensed by the state after taking exams. Although states differ in what they call different levels of the profession and in the board that oversees them, your first line of defense is to make sure that your current or potential accountant is licensed.

You can do that with a telephone call to the state board. To find out if your accountant has had any disciplinary action taken against him, you should put your request in writing.

The board is obliged to give you the full record, although it will not inform you of *pending* disciplinary action.

Don't confuse the state licensing board with the American Institute of Certified Public Accountants (AICPA). This is a national professional group with state chapters. Your accountant's being a member is a good sign, since in many states the organization does quality reviews and self-policing of its membership. Here, too, you will not be told about disciplinary actions.

If your accountant is a member of AICPA, ask if he or she subscribes to the AICPA "Division of Firms," a special membership category. Those accountants who join the Division of Firms voluntarily submit their records for regular auditing and inspection by other Division of Firms members. The process helps keep accountants up-to-date and honest.

You should do your own review of your accountant. Check with other members of your profession or business whom you respect and find out if any use your accountant. If they don't, find out why not. The firm may not be expert in your field, which should give you pause—or it may have a bad track record, which you should definitely know about.

Source: Doug Stives, partner in Curchin & Co., Certified Public Accountants, Red Bank, NJ, and past president of the New Jersey chapter of the American Institute of Certified Public Accountants.

How to Cut Your State Taxes

Most state income tax systems are tied directly to the federal income tax. In calculating your state tax, you start with your federal adjusted gross or taxable income. Any of those things that you can do to cut your tax at the federal level will pass through to your state income tax return.

But—there are still a few ways in which you can directly cut your state tax bill.

•Move to a state that has no income tax or one that has a low income tax. No-tax states: Alaska, Florida, New Hampshire, Nevada, South Dakota, Texas, Washington, and Wyoming. (Tennessee taxes interest and dividend income but not earned income.) Low-tax states: Illinois and Pennsylvania.

To change your state for tax purposes, you have to show an intent to move your "domicile" from where you currently live to a new state. For purposes of state income taxation, your domicile is the place to which you intend to return. What state tax officials look for in determining that your domicile has changed...

•Buying residential real estate in the new state.

•Selling the home in which you currently live.

•Changing your voter registration to the new state.

•Joining clubs in the new state.

•Developing business relationships in the new state.

Opportunity: If you do change states, consider selling assets on the installment basis to shift taxable income from your old state to the new one. You may be able to arrange the sale so you accept part of the gain when you're a resident in a taxing state, and have most of the gain recognized when you're a resident of a nontaxing state. This would be the best way to sell your business, for example.

Caution: A handful of states take the position that if a taxpayer is leaving the state, the whole gain on an installment sale is triggered for tax purposes—if the gain was generated from the sale of assets in that state.

Important: Check your state's position on installment sales before you go ahead and make such an arrangement.

Complications: Changing states for tax purposes is not a simple matter.

Here are some of the complications you must take into account...

•Some states tax retirement income generated by work in that state even when the taxpayer has moved to another state. New York is one such state, and California is another. Other states, however, don't tax retirement income at all. Illinois is one such state.

•If you continue to earn income from a business activity in your former state, that state has the right to tax that income. *Example:* You get rental income from real estate.

•The state you move to might have other taxes that compensate for the fact that it has no income tax. It might have a steep property tax or sales tax, or an intangibles tax (a tax on securities), like Florida. If a state doesn't have an income tax, it probably means that it's much more dependent on other sources of taxation than a state that has an income tax. *Key question:* What will your consumption pattern be in the state you're planning to move to?

•Maximize your tax credits from investments in flow-through entities, such as partnerships and S corporations. More and more of these investments (tax shelters) tend to be multistate investments, especially if they're in real estate. States other than your residency state will impose tax on the income generated in their state. You're entitled to a tax credit in your residency state for taxes paid to another state.

Self-defense: Check with the entity to make sure you're getting all the credits you're entitled to.

Important: Be sure the entity you're investing in is meeting its responsibility of filing returns in every state where it earns income.

•Maximize your investment in municipal bonds. Many states take a position that bonds issued by municipalities within the state are free from state income tax. When you're shopping around for municipal bonds (which generally are free from federal income tax), look for those that are eligible for state tax exemption. Take the bond's state tax-free status into consideration when comparing its after-tax yield with a taxable bond.

If you're investing in a tax-exempt bond fund, look for one that specializes in bonds eligible for exemption in your state. General funds, which include bonds from other states, are not totally exempt from state taxes. Check the fund's prospectus.

Source: J. Thomas Johnson, national director of state and local taxes, Grant Thornton, CPAs, 700 Prudential Plaza, 130 E. Randolph St., Chicago 60601.

Banks & Credit Cards

Tricks Banks Play With Interest Rates

Banks teach their loan officers a number of strategies to get an extra 1/4% or even 1/2% from borrowers. *Recognize some of their tricks:*

•Doing the negotiating at the bank, which is familiar territory to the banker, is intimidating to the borrower.

•Not mentioning the rate at all, but simply filling it in on the note.

•"Since you need the money today, let's write it up at X%. Then we can talk later about changing it." The banker hopes you'll never bring it up again. *He* certainly won't.

•Flat statement: "The rate for this type of loan is X%." (Never true except for small consumer loans. There is always room for you to negotiate.)

•Postponing the rate discussion as long as possible, hoping borrower will weaken under deadline pressure.

•Ego-building. Bank president stops by during negotiations.

•Talking constantly about how little the interest costs after taxes. And comparing it with finance company rates, secondary mortgage rates, or the cost of equity capital.

The banker looks at the company's account as a package, including loans, average balances maintained, and fees for service. *Borrower options:* Trade off higher average balances for a lower interest rate on borrowings or vice versa.

The borrower is at a disadvantage because he probably negotiates a loan only once a year or less, while the banker does this full-time. So prepare carefully for negotiations.

Good tactics for the borrower:

•Ask interest-rate questions early—in your office, not his. Don't volunteer suggestions.

•Negotiate everything as a package—rate, repayment schedule, collateral, compensating balances. The banker's strategy will be to try to nail down everything else and then negotiate the interest rate when the borrower has no more leverage and no room to maneuver.

•Be prepared with an expression of surprise and shock, even rehearse it before a mirror. React that way when the banker mentions the interest rate, no matter what the figure is.

Source: Lawrence T. Jilk, Jr., executive vice president, National Bank of Boyertown, Pa., in *The Journal of Commercial Bank Lending.*

What Banks Don't Tell You

•Banks like to advertise their *effective annual yield,* whereas money-market funds are legally permitted to advertise only the simple interest rates. The long-standing rule inadvertently conceals the fact that money-market funds *do* compound interest on a daily basis. If a bank and a money-market fund pay the *same rate,* the bank will *appear* to offer more by advertising the *effective rate.*

•Some banks say they let you draw on all checks immediately, provided you put up another bank account as collateral. *Catch:* If a check backed by a six-month certificate bounces, the bank can break into the certificate before maturity. If this happens, you will have to pay an interest penalty. *Protection:* Pick a bank that will allow you time to *cover* a bounced check before it takes money from your time deposit. Be *sure* your bank has this policy before you decide to use a time deposit as collateral.

•Don't bite if the bank offers you a big savings in return for a lump-sum payoff of the old low-interest mortgage on your home. *The catch:* The discount "bonus" comes from principal—not interest—and is taxable income. You will gain a greater return on your money if you set aside the amount sought by the bank and invest it yourself.

•Checks dated more than six months ago are usually not cashable, no matter how much money the issuer has in the bank. (*Exception:* US Treasury checks are valid indefinitely.)

•If the amount written on the check in words is different from the amount written in numbers, the bank will pay the sum shown *in words.*

•Be careful when endorsing checks. To prevent loss of money when sending checks by mail for deposit, write "For Deposit Only" above your signature on the back. That limits the endorsement. An endorsed check with nothing but a signature is the same as cash and can be used by anybody if it's lost or stolen.

Safeguards for Safe-Deposit Boxes

Valuables stored in bank safe-deposit boxes are not automatically protected against loss through burglary, flood, or fire. To be compensated for missing valuables, depositors must initiate lawsuits against the bank. The chances of winning are very, very slim.

Safeguards: Buy insurance for the contents of the boxes even though reimbursement levels are low. And most negotiable items, such as securities, bank notes, gold, coins, and cash, are not covered.

Alternative: Store stocks and bonds at the brokerage house where they were purchased. These firms have a legal and financial responsibility to guard securities stored with them.

Another option: Open a custody account with a bank. The bank holds securities and other assets in its vault. It collects and credits all dividends, but does not manage the assets. The bank will replace any asset in the vault that is lost, stolen, or harmed. Charges are generally based on the size of the account and the composition of the holdings.

When the Bank Can't Bounce a Check

The bank may have to honor a check if it takes too long to bounce it. Uniform Commercial Code requires that the bank take some action by midnight of the business day after it receives the check. But the bank gets more time if there's an emergency beyond its control—for example, a computer breakdown.

Checks Marked "Payment in Full"

If there's no dispute as to the amount, a check tendered for less than the amount due and marked "payment in full" (or the like) may be cashed without prejudicing the right to recover the balance.

If there's a bona fide dispute as to the amount owing, the creditor must be wary. *Alternatives:* Reject the check and demand full payment. *Or:* Accept the check but run the risk that payment will be deemed to have settled the disputed claim for the lesser amount. It's easy enough for a debtor who wants to pay less than the amount for which he's billed to create a dispute on the basis of quantitative or qualitative deficiencies in the goods or services supplied.

Stamp the check with a statement to the effect that "Check is accepted without prejudice and with full reservation of all rights under Section 1-207 of the Uniform Commercial Code." The effectiveness of this technique is untested in the courts, but it may help to protect a creditor's rights and provide leverage in a settlement.

How to Deposit An Unsigned Check

Write or type the word *over* on the line where the signature would normally appear. On the back, type *lack of signature guaranteed*...and add your company's name and your name and title. Then sign. This guarantees your bank that you'll take back the check as a charge against your account if it isn't honored. Most banks will then process the check and remit the funds. This saves you the trouble of returning the check to your customer for signature.

Source: *Credit & Financial Management*, 475 Park Ave. S., New York 10016.

Credit Cards: Beating the System

Credit cards have become a way of life for most Americans. However, very few people realize the unnecessary costs they incur by not utilizing their cards to their advantage or by not choosing the least expensive card to begin with.

Determine which card is best for you. Banks offering VISA or MasterCard services have a wide variety of fees and interest charges. Some levy a $35 charge, while others will nick you for only $20. Moreover, interest charges for goods purchased range from 18% to 22%. And some banks charge interest from the date of purchase, while others charge no interest if you pay your monthly bill on time.

Watch out, too, for bank cards that bill on a 24-day cycle, which means customers receive 14 bills per year. If you are used to paying all your bills once a month, one of those 14 could easily get delayed in the shuffle. Then you will be charged interest on the missed bill and get a reputation for being a slow payer.

Even if the credit terms and service charges are to your liking, find out if there is any time limit on them. Some banks offer attractive deals as part of a special promotion that expires after nine months or a year. Take advantage of such offers—but be ready to switch over to another bank card if it is less expensive once the promotion expires.

Credit cards can also be used as a bargaining chip to receive a discount from a merchant. Merchants typically pay a fee of 2%–7% of your charge when you use your credit card. With an American Express or Diners Club card, they may have to wait a while to get paid. It may be to the advantage of the merchant to go along with your suggestion of a 5% discount if you pay cash.

Another way to beat the system: Take a cash advance on your credit card and pay directly for goods and services, rather than charge them, if bank-interest charges are less for cash advances. If you are already being charged interest for merchandise purchases, take a cash advance and switch the balance due to the lower rate.

If no interest charge has yet been levied, then time the cash advance to a day or two before the bill would be past due and pay off the merchandise portion of the bill. *Reason for the timing maneuver:* Cash advances are charged interest from the day they are taken. Multiple credit cards come in handy if you want to go to the limit of allowable cash advances on each without having to use your card to purchase merchandise at high rates.

If you have gotten in over your head, it may be best to take out a consumer loan to pay off a number of credit-card bills. Although the consumer loan rate may not be much cheaper than the credit-card cash advance rate, it can be significantly cheaper than the card's basic interest rate on merchandise purchases. In addition, since bank credit-card payments are based on a 24-month term, one big advantage to consolidating your debts with a 36-month consumer loan is lower monthly payments.

Source: Edward Mendlowitz, a partner with Mendlowitz Weitsen, CPAs, New York.

Stretching Due Dates on Bills

Due dates on bills can be stretched—but not far—without risk. Typical grace periods: Telephone companies, eight days. Gas and electric utilities, 10 days. Banks and finance companies, 10 days. Even after a late charge is imposed on an unpaid bill, your credit rating should be safe for 30 days.

Source: Terry Blaney, president of Consumer Credit Counseling Service of Houston and the Gulf Cost area.

Twelve Ways to Avoid Being Ripped Off by Your Bank

1. Never borrow on a typical installment-loan basis. These loans are front-end loaded. That is, you pay interest on the original balance of the loan through the entire term of the loan, even though you are reducing the amount you owe every month through your repayments.

2. Never buy credit life and disability insurance from a bank.

3. Negotiate before taking out a mortgage. Don't assume that such items as interest rates, "points" (prepaid interest), and closing costs are set in stone. You have to speak up.

4. Consider paying off the principal on your mortgage early.

5. Don't allow the bank to force you to make payments into a bank escrow fund for your home insurance and property taxes.

6. Never borrow through your credit cards.

7. Know the pitfalls of bank safe-deposit boxes. Bank vaults are not impervious to break-ins, fires, or floods. If anything happens, the contents of the box may not be insured under the bank's insurance policy.

8. Avoid automatic teller machines (ATMs). Banks duped consumers into using ATMs by telling them it would cut labor costs by eliminating expensive human tellers. But now that consumers are hooked, banks want to make these ATMs profit centers. It's a rare bank these days that doesn't charge customers for the privilege of using such machines. Furthermore, ATMs can be dangerous to your physical as well as your financial health. Despite repeated robberies, most banks do not provide security guards for customers using after-hour ATMs.

9. Beware of overdraft checking. This service allows you to write checks for more than you have in your account. It's based on customers' fear that their checks will bounce. While it may sound like a bargain, overdraft checking is often nothing more than an expensive way to get you deeper into debt.

10. Avoid bank Individual Retirement Accounts (IRAs). While IRAs are a fine idea, banks rarely offer the best deal in town. Usually, their rates on certificates of deposit are not competitive with other institutions, and may be one to three percentage points below the market.

11. Do preventive maintenance on your personal bank account. It's always smart to get on a first-name basis with the manager and several tellers of the branch of your local bank.

12. Use a small bank rather than a big one. At big banks, the attitude often is, *We do it our way or we don't do it at all.* But smaller banks tend to be more flexible and rarely have a large bureaucracy for you to contend with.

Source: Edward F. Mrkvicka, Jr., author of *The Bank Book: How to Revoke Your Bank's License to Steal,* HarperCollins, 10 E. 53 St., New York 10022.

The 20 Safest Banks in The US—and the Lemons

The safest big banks in the country are those that have shaken off their bad loans and have the lowest percentage of nonperforming assets as a percentage of assets. During 1991, 24 big banks managed to keep deadbeat loans at 1% *or less*—of total assets.

Top of the list:

United Missouri Bancshares/.2%
Israel Discount Bank/.3%
State Street Boston/.4%
Bancorp Hawaii/.4%
First Citizens Bancshares/.5%
Commerce Bancshares/.6%
First Virginia Banks/.6%
First Alabama Bancshares/.6%
Republic New York/.6%
First Hawaiian/.6%
J. P. Morgan/.6%
Northern Trust/.7%
Comerica/.8%
Firstar/.9%
Manufacturers National/.9%
Wachovia/.9%
LaSalle National/.9%
Marshall & Ilsley/.9%
Central Fidelity Banks/1%
First Tennessee National/1%
Central Bancshares of the South/1%
NBD Bancorp/1%
West One Bancorp/1%
Norwest/1%

The average percentage of nonperforming assets as a percent of assets among the top 100 US banks was 3.3%. During 1991, there were 10 banks with the highest percentage of deadbeat loans.

Bottom of the list:

MNC Financial/10.2%
Midlantic/10%
Marine Midland Banks/7.7%
First City Bancorp of Texas/6.7%
Citicorp/6.4%
Riggs National/6%
Security Pacific/5.7%
Chase Manhattan/5.4%
Baybanks/5.3%
Bank of Tokyo Trust/5%

Source: Standard & Poor's Compustat Service, Inc.

Health

The Smart Way to Pick A Health Club

A health club or sports center is a good deal only if you can use it often and safely. *What to look for:*

•Convenience to either your home or your office (15 minutes or less away).

•Hours that suit your schedule.

•A variety of equipment and facilities so that you can enjoy both aerobic workouts—and strength training.

•Trained staff (college degrees in physical education or certification from the American College of Sports Medicine or the Institute of Aerobic Research) to help you set realistic and measurable fitness goals.

•Trained staff to supervise your safe mastery of the equipment and your step-by-step increase in resistance or repetitions within a program designed for your individual needs.

•Enough equipment in good, working order so that you don't have to wait to work out at the hours you are free.

•A clean and well-maintained environment.

•A congenial atmosphere where you feel comfortable with the other members.

•A three-month or less trial membership.

•A refund policy if you become disabled or move.

If a health club meets these criteria, you will likely use your membership to get and stay fit. And such a club will justify its fee. The best bargains in health clubs are often at the local Y.

Health clubs are now regulated in 32 states, but the regulations vary and don't always protect the public from a club's going into bankruptcy. To protect yourself, avoid clubs where:

•You are pressured to sign up that day. You should be able to take a contract home and study it.

•You are offered a lifetime membership for a hefty fee (this is illegal in many states).

•The staff has no recognized credentials. You can injure yourself by using the workout equipment in the club incorrectly.

•Pool areas are not kept clean and free from mildew and mold (you should be able to see the bottom of the pool if it is properly treated).

•You see equipment not being used because it is out of service.

•The Better Business Bureau has complaints against the club.

•You don't get good vibes from talking to the other members when you visit.

Exercises That Can Hurt You

You should be careful in selecting an exercise plan. Correct breathing and posture during exercise are essential. Improper exercising can cause or aggravate injuries: Even basic exercises can be dangerous:

•*Toe-touching:* Doing this with the knees in a locked position and with a rapid bouncing action places tremendous pressure on the lumbar vertebrae. This could result in lower-back pain. Allow your knees to bend slightly, and remain in a hanging-over position for three complete slow, deep breaths. Then straighten slowly. Repeat this three times. Do it without bouncing.

•*Leg lifts:* Performing these while lying on your back and raising both legs at the same time can cause the pelvis to rotate and lead to swayback (the problem of lower-back lordosis). Eliminate this exercise.

•*Sit-ups:* Doing these with straight legs can also contribute to an increased curvature of the lower back. To give the abdominal muscles a real workout, bend your knees, keep your feet flat on the floor, fold your arms over your chest, and curl up to only a 30° angle from the floor.

•*Deep knee bends:* These can cause injury to knee cartilage. Bending the knees so that they are directly over the feet and the thighs are parallel to the floor will not cause injury.

The important thing to remember is that any repeated movement done in an unnatural position can create problems. Two key areas of the body to be concerned with are the knees and the lower back. If an exercise is painful, perhaps you are doing it improperly, or it is too advanced for you. *Or:* It may simply be a dangerous exercise.

Medicines That Can Hurt You When You Exercise

Drugs and exercise can be a hazardous combination. *Aspirin* can mask the pain that should tell you to stop. *Antihistamines* can cause drowsiness and strain the heart and muscles. *Decongestants* raise overall blood pressure. *Diuretics* can lead to dehydration and cramping. *Tranquilizers,* besides robbing you of your competitive edge, dull your perception of pain. *Best:* Take a new drug at least twice and gauge your reaction *before* adding the stress of vigorous exercise. And never combine different drugs with exercise without consulting your doctor.

Source: Dr. Richard H. Dominguez, co-medical director, Sports Performance and Rehabilitation Institute, Carol Stream, IL.

Exercises to Do in the Car

(1) *Double chin:* Lift chin slightly and open and close mouth as though chewing. (2) *Flabby neck:* Move head toward right shoulder while looking straight ahead at the road. Return head to center, then toward left shoulder. (3) *Pot belly:* Sit straight with spine against back seat. Pull stomach in and hold breath for count of 5. Relax, then repeat. The exercise also relieves tension and helps fight sleepiness.

Working Off a Big Meal Is Easier Than You Think

Exercising soon after eating is an efficient way to burn off excess calories. *Reason:* Since both eating a good meal and exercising *raise* your body's metabolic rate, you use up more calories exercising *after* a meal than before one. (Conversely, cutting back on calories *lowers* your metabolism and makes you work harder to burn off what you do eat.) *Minimum requirement for working off a meal:* A 20-minute walk within 45 minutes of eating.

Source: David Levitsky and Eva Obarzanek, Division of Nutritional Sciences, Cornell University.

Vitamin E Warning

Research on E's toxic effects is sketchy, but the findings suggest some problems: headaches, nausea, fatigue and giddiness, blurred vision, chapped lips and mouth inflammation, low blood sugar, increased tendency to bleed, reduced sexual function. Ironically, one of the claims of vitamin E proponents is that it heightens sexual potency.

Source: Dr. Victor Herbert, *Nutrition Cultism: Facts and Fictions*, George F. Stickley Co., Philadelphia.

Vitamin C and Aspirin

These substances should *not* be taken together. Studies at Southern Illinois University indicate that combined *heavy doses* produce excessive stomach irritation, which could lead to ulcers (especially for those with a history of stomach problems).

Pros and Cons of Vasectomy

According to studies, vasectomies have no effect on the production of testosterone or other hormones. The body still produces both sperm (which is reabsorbed by the body) and seminal fluid (which is ejaculated).

Vasectomies are considered so safe and simple that they're generally performed under local anesthetic in a doctor's office or in a clinic. The doctor makes one or two incisions in the scrotum through which each sperm-carrying tube (*vas deferens*) can be lifted out, cut, and closed, thus blocking the passage of sperm. The surgery is usually covered by Blue Shield or another private medical insurance. If it is performed on Friday afternoon, most men can go back to work on Monday. Best then to wear an athletic supporter and avoid heavy labor for a week to 10 days. There may be some discomfort for several days. Usually ice packs and aspirin provide all the relief that is needed. Contraception is still necessary for the first 10 to 12 ejaculations after a vasectomy—until two samples of semen, generally taken a week or two apart, show no sperm.

Physical Aftereffects

• *Sperm antibodies* develop in about 50% of vasectomized men. One type of antibody immobilizes sperm. The other causes sperm to agglutinate (clump together). These antibodies may prevent restoration of fertility in men whose vasectomies are later reversed. But it is not yet known for what length of time these sperm antibodies go on being produced and under what conditions the body stops producing them.

• *Increased cholesterol and atherosclerotic plaque.* The results of an experiment on monkeys at the Oregon Primate Research Center, which concluded that vasectomies produced increased cholesterol and atherosclerotic plaque, were widely publicized. However, there were only five monkeys in the experimental group, and the monkeys' diet contained *twice the cholesterol* found in an ordinary human diet. More recent studies belie the connection between vasectomies and atherosclerotic build-up in men.

Reversibility

Vasectomies *can* be reversed—*sometimes.* Although major surgery is involved, microsurgical vasovasotomy (reconnecting the tubes) is the technique used when remarriage or another major life change makes a man decide to father children again. Some doctors claim a 40%–50% success rate on vasectomy reversals (provided the wife is fertile, of course). This figure will probably rise as microsurgical techniques continue to become more sophisticated.

More Information: Association for Voluntary Sterilization, 708 Third Ave., New York 10017.

Headache Relief Without Drugs

Relief from incapacitating tension, vascular, and migraine headaches is possible without drugs, using a self-administered form of acupuncture known as *acupressure.*

The technique: Exert *very heavy* thumbnail pressure (painful pressure) successively on nerves lying just below the surface of the skin at key points in the hands and wrists. As with acupuncture, no one's sure *why* it works.

Pressure points to try:

•The triangle of flesh between the thumb and index finger on the back of your hands (thumb side of bone, near the middle of the second metacarpal in the index finger).

•Just above the protruding bone on the thumb side of your wrist.

When Painkillers Cause More Pain

Overreliance on aspirin or acetaminophen can make matters worse for as many as 12 million Americans who suffer from chronic muscle-contraction headaches—about 25% of all severe headaches. *Trap:* Rebound headaches caused by analgesics.

Overuse of painkillers stymies the body's natural painkilling mechanisms, increasing pain and encouraging sufferers to take more medication—causing still more pain. Most common in those who average five to six aspirin or acetaminophen tablets a day, the problem can also occur in those who take as few as two daily.

To break the cycle, gradually cut the number of pain medications taken. *Helpful:* Biofeedback, antidepressants. Improvement usually begins within a month.

Source: Alan Rapoport, MD, director, New England Center for Headache, Cos Cob, CT.

Sexual Side Effects of Widely Used Medicines

Many illnesses can themselves cause impotence and lack of libido, but in other cases, it is the medication that brings on changes in sexual desire and capability. Research in this area is scanty, and the sexual side effects of many drugs are not universal. Discuss your situation with your doctor. However, the following drugs are known to have affected the sex lives of many who take them regularly:

High Blood Pressure Medicines

•Esimil and Ismelin (guanethidine) may impair ejaculation and cause lack of potency in men.

•Aldomet, Aldoclor, and Aldoril (methlydopa) can decrease sexual desire and make holding an erection difficult for men. In rare cases, they cause a man's breasts to develop.

•Diupres, Exna-R, Rau-Sed, Regroton, Salutensin, Ser-Ap-Es, and Serpasil (reserpine) can cause reduced libido and potency, delayed ejaculation, and enlarged breasts.

•Catapres (clonidine) can produce impotence in men and failure to achieve orgasm in women.

•Eutonyl and Eutron (pargyline) may bring on impotence, delayed ejaculation, or delayed orgasm.

•Inderal and Inderide (propranolol) rarely cause side effects, although difficulty with erections have been reported.

Digestive-Tract Drugs

Many of the older, commonly prescribed ulcer drugs such as Banthine, Bentyl, Donnagel, Donnatel, Pamine, Pathibamate, and Pro-Banthine have been associated with sexual problems. The more recent medication Tagamet (cimetidine) has been reported to reduce male potency and enlarge breasts when given in very high doses.

Tranquilizers

Librium and Valium have quite opposite effects on different individuals. For some, these drugs reduce inhibitions and increase sexual desire. In other cases, they decrease libido.

Birth-Control Pills

Regardless of brand, the sexual effects vary among women. Many report increased libido, which may simply be a release from the fear of pregnancy. Some women claim decreased sexual desire while taking the pill, which may be caused by the drug's effect on hormonal regulation.

Antidepressant Drugs

Depression itself often causes a lack of interest in sex. Antidepressant drugs sometimes increase libido and sometimes decrease it. Other sexual side effects vary widely and are not well recorded. Possible problems include impotence, testicular swelling, breast enlargement and milk secretion, impaired ejaculation in men, and delayed orgasm in women.

Antipsychotic Drugs

Many medications used to treat mental illness have adverse sexual side effects that have not been fully documented. Among the symptoms are impotence, difficulty in ejaculation, irregular menstruation, abnormal lactation, increased and decreased sexual desire, and even false positive pregnancy tests.

Source: Joe Graedon, a pharmacologist and the author of *The People's Pharmacy* and *The People's Pharmacy-2*, Avon Books, New York.

Getting a Good Night's Sleep Without Pills

Sleep problems—from real insomnia to occasional restless slumber—can be cured.

The first step in the cure is to become aware that you're not alone—and that something can be done.

Occasional insomniacs usually contribute to their problem by worrying that theirs is a serious problem—and a symptom of even more sleep problems in the future. Occasional means anything from one sleepless night a week to one a year. In most cases, sufferers should dismiss these symptoms. They are usually caused by a specific and temporary stress or anxiety.

How do you know when your *occasional* insomnia has become a *chronic* disorder?

To be a chronic problem, the loss of sleep must have a real effect on your *daytime* functioning. A good question to ask yourself is, *What would I be doing differently during the day if I were getting eight hours of sleep a night?* In other words, what benefit would being able to sleep bring you?

Sometimes a person is simply not sleeping as much as he/she *thinks* he should, but his daytime functioning is not adversely affected. In these cases, the individual is probably trying to sleep more hours than he needs to.

Prescription for the occasional insomniac: Condition your sleep environment. Learn to associate your bed and your bedroom with sleep.

How to do it:

•Pay attention to bedroom conditions, such as light, heat, noise. Shut off telephones if necessary. Keep temperature cool (around 68°). Make sure your mattress and your sleep clothing are comfortable.

•If you don't fall asleep right away, get up, leave the bedroom, and do something else. Don't lie awake thinking about it. Staying in bed for hours trying to get to sleep accentuates the problem. You begin to associate your bed and bedroom with *trying to sleep* instead of with sleeping.

•Stick to a regular bedtime schedule. Go to bed at the same time every night—weekdays and weekends. Some insomniacs have the idea they'll catch up on missed sleep on the weekends. You can't do it. Trying to do this simply disrupts your biological rhythms.

Other popular sleep inducers or aids:

•Sleeping pills. Doctor-prescribed sedatives are very useful in *temporary* situations where a particular emotional or physical upset is the cause of the insomnia. *Problem:* Tendency to become dependent on them and a worsening of the quality of sleep as more pills are used.

How to handle pills: Use for no more than a week or two. Expect sleep to be very disturbed the first night or two after stopping the pills. That's perfectly normal. Expect it and accept it.

•Nonprescription, over-the-counter sleeping pills are absolutely useless. Studies have shown "sugar pills" to be just as effective.

•*Exercise.* Early in the day is okay. Late in the evening is too stimulating. *Exception to the rule:* Sexual activity, within a comfortable relationship where no tension or anxiety exists, is helpful.

•*Caffeine.* Coffee, tea, and soft drinks act as stimulants. Avoid completely.

•*Alcohol.* May help you get to sleep but interferes with the quality of sleep. Wears off after several hours.

•Widely advertised insomnia cures such as vibrating beds, prerecorded cassette tapes, and sleep masks are fine if they relax you.

Source: Dr. Frank Zorick, former clinical director of the sleep disorder center at Cincinnati Veterans Administration Hospital and the University of Cincinnati.

Facts and Fallacies About Dental Care

•Bad teeth *don't* cause headaches, bursitis, or anything like that. But jaw and tooth pains may be "referred" pains that originate in other areas.

•A tooth knocked out in an accident *can* be saved. When a child falls and loses a tooth, pick it up—but don't stop to clean it. Wrap it in a wet cloth and take it and the child to the dentist as quickly as possible. Reimplantation works best with children (sometimes with adults, too).

•Playing the trumpet or trombone can correct a bad bite. However, playing the flute or piccolo can make it worse. Playing the saxophone can work either way.

•Pain perception is less in the morning than in the afternoon, according to recent research. *Suggestion:* Schedule dental appointments early in the day.

•If you don't want to pay for a crown for a badly decayed tooth, ask for a filling with reinforcement pins. This does the job almost as well at a fraction of the cost.

•Toothbrushes: Use two or more in rotation so that they can dry out properly. *Soft* nylon is best. Natural-bristle brushes take longer to dry. If it isn't used properly, a brush can damage gum tissue because the bristles are too firm and coarse. Angled brushes may help in reaching some areas. *Caution:* Too-vigorous brushing can wear grooves in tooth enamel. When used correctly, a toothbrush will not abrade tissues or teeth. And hardness of the bristles is not as significant as the way the brush is used and the time spent brushing.

•Dental floss. *Unwaxed* floss is better because it absorbs particles.

•Flushing devices (such as a Water Pik): If used with too much pressure, the device can damage tissue, force debris into periodontal pockets, and cause inflammation and infection. *Recommendation:* Use at half the recommended pressure.

How to Get VIP Treatment in a Hospital

The first thing an admitting clerk does when you're brought into a hospital is slip a plastic tag with an identity number onto your wrist. From that point on, like it or not, you are a number to most of the hospital staff.

Being a number instead of a name can be an awful shock. It means that you may be treated as if you have no identity—except for your symptoms, vital signs, and medical treatment.

Fortunately, there are steps you can take to improve that treatment. And those steps, if successful, will not only make you feel more comfortable and human during your hospital visit, they could dramatically affect your state of health by the time you're ready to be discharged. In fact, it may be the issue that determines whether you leave alive or dead.

Think of a hospital as a huge, complex hotel—however, one that dispenses more than food, entertainment, and lodging.

As you know, a hospital dispenses both lifesaving and life-threatening services. A moment's inattention at a hospital can lead to tragedy.

So how do you get the hospital to treat you like a person instead of a number?

In general, you've got to use the same techniques you use in other aspects of your personal and business life. The key word is *assertiveness.* That's not to say you should complain and be demanding—although, as you'll see, that may be necessary under certain circumstances.

Finding the Right Doctor

The first step in getting VIP treatment in a hospital should be taken long before you're admitted—and that's finding a doctor who can provide the leverage you'll need. You want someone with more than an MD after his name.

Every community has a clique of doctors who have political clout. Usually, these are physicians who serve on the local hospital's board of directors. Be aware, however, that a doctor with clout doesn't necessarily have the skills or any other attributes that make a physician a superior healer. Do you want such a person as your personal physician? Generally speaking, the answer is no, but there are exceptions. If you're satisfied that such a doctor can serve double-duty, so to speak, then you need go no further.

The drawbacks: Aside from the possibility that such a doctor may be more expert in a boardroom than in an operating room, there are other potential problems.

The most serious: He/she may be more interested in keeping his professional calendar and the institution's beds filled than in your welfare. Of course, there are ways to get around that. If he wants to admit you to the hospital for treatment and there is doubt in your mind about this decision, ask for a consultation.

Generally speaking, it's always wise to get a consultation for any complex medical procedure—and the likelihood is that the procedure he's recommending is relatively complex if he wants to hospitalize you. So by asking for a consultation, you're not showing lack of faith in your doctor.

Caveat: However, there have been many instances in which doctors are annoyed when a patient announces that he/she would like a consultation or a second opinion. If you ever face a less-than-cooperative response to such a request, it would be prudent to seek out another doctor immediately. It's well within your rights to consult with as many physicians as you wish.

To guarantee better attention once you know that you're going to spend time in a hospital, make a date with the hospital administrator.

He/she may or may not be a doctor—but in any case, he is a businessman, so you can be sure he speaks the same language as you. Introduce yourself. Tell him that you're a little concerned about your hospital stay and you'd appreciate it if he'd take a personal interest in your case.

He'll get the message, and in all likelihood, he'll take steps to be sure that you're well cared for. Now that you've made your presence known, he will probably, out of courtesy, call the head of nursing and the admitting office and tell them that you are coming to the hospital and they should be expecting you. It's just such words, without pressure, that may make all the difference in the way you're subsequently treated.

Once You're in the Hospital

Even if you've failed or haven't had the time to take the above steps, there are still things you can do to ensure good, if not VIP, treatment.

If you're not physically up to it, your spouse or a friend or relative may have to help you, but if you're feeling well enough, you can take the following steps yourself:

•During the admission procedure, ask what rooms are available. You may prefer a private room, or for the sake of company, you may want to share a room with someone else. If you do want to share, ask about your potential roommate's medical status to be sure that you can deal with his/her illness.

•After settling into your room, ask to see the dietitian. Explain that you understand that the hospital is not a hotel, but within reasonable bounds, and limited by doctor's orders, there are foods that you do and do not like. Itemize them. If you present your request with tact, the dietitian will probably try to meet your reasonable requests.

•Go out of your way to be polite to the nursing staff. They are your lifeline. If the nurses take a dislike to you, the recuperation period will not be smooth.

•It's not tacky to provide small favors, such as a box of candy, and even flowers, on each of the three nursing shifts: the 8 A.M. to 4 P.M., the 4 P.M. to midnight, and the midnight to 8 A.M. Don't offer a gratuity until you're ready to be discharged. Nurses are professionals, and most would resent the offer. But if you received extra-special care from a nurse during your stay, a tasteful gift isn't inappropriate.

•Make it clear that you'd like to know what medication or treatment is being given to you *beforehand.* This will require a discussion with your doctor. Most doctors work on the premise that patients don't want to know too much and only provide information as it's necessary or if the patient specifically requests it.

Unfortunately, mistakes are made now and then, but if you ask the nurse "What are these pills?" or "What exactly will you be doing to me?" and she has orders from your doctor to provide that information on request, it gives the staff the opportunity to double-check what they are doing and gives you a chance to say "Wait a minute!" if an obvious error is being made.

If you're not happy with your care, explain your complaint to the nurse firmly and politely. If that gets you no place, ask to speak to the head nurse. And if that fails, you may have to speak to either your doctor or the hospital administrator. Usually, when you reach that level, and you're not being unreasonable, steps will be taken to satisfy your complaint and resolve your problem.

How to Learn About Medical Discoveries Before Your Doctor Does

In this age of information, it's possible—with a little persistence—to keep up with all the experimental work that is going on in the disease or condition in which you are interested. You then bring this information to the attention of your doctor.

The first line of attack is to find a support group of families and patients who share your interest, whether it is the Heart Association, the Arthritis Foundation.

These groups make it their business to keep up with all the work worldwide that involves their disease. Many help finance research and also publish their own newsletters.

Ask your doctor for the names of support groups for your condition. Or go to the library and ask a research librarian how to find the type of organization that interests you.

In many libraries, the research librarians will also do a computer search of medical databases for your disease. You can then look up articles that seem pertinent or pay for the library to print them out from the database.

Join the support group for your disease. Subscribe to its publications. When you find out about research or treatments that seem pertinent, bring them to the attention of your doctor.

Source: Bruce Yaffe, MD, an internist in private practice in New York, who also consults with medical publications.

Understanding Hospital Talk

A hospital patient may have considerable difficulty understanding some of the jargon used by

nurses and other hospital personnel. Here are what some commonly used terms mean:
NPO—Sign placed by the bed of a patient who is not to get anything to eat or drink.
Emesis basin—Pan brought to patients who are sick to their stomach.
Ambulate—Take the patient for a walk.
Force fluids—Encourage intake of lots of liquid.
Void—Urinate.
IV—Intravenous.
OOB—Out of bed.
IPPB—Intermittent Positive Pressure Breathing machine to aid breathing.
hs—Medication before sleep.
BP—Blood pressure.
HR—Heart rate.
Medication schedule:
qid—4 times a day.
tid—3 times a day.
bid—2 times a day.
od or *qd*—Once a day.
qod—Every other day.

Questions to Ask a Surgeon

To protect against unnecessary surgery, ask the physician hard questions *beforehand.*

•What are the risks?

•What is the mortality rate for this operation?

•How long will it take to recover?

•What is the likelihood of complications? What sort, if any?

•Are there alternative ways to treat this condition?*

•How many people have you seen with similar symptoms who have chosen *not* to have surgery?

•How many of these operations have you done in the past year?

**Always get a second opinion.*

How to Get Fast Emergency Medical Care

These days, most emergency rooms (ERs) are characterized by confusion and chaos.

Problem: Money alone won't get you better treatment. *Much more effective:* Inside knowledge...knowledge of how the system works and how you can make it work for you.

First step: The triage ("sorting") nurse will assess the priority of your medical need. This person will look you over and then ask several questions. Be prepared to give your medical history succinctly and descriptively.

Planning: Before a medical emergency strikes, prepare a card that lists your medical history, including allergies or other chronic conditions and previous operations or serious illnesses. Keep it handy and, in an emergency, take it to the hospital.

Organize your thoughts so that you're able to describe, clearly and accurately, symptoms, time of onset, and medications taken. Don't draw conclusions or give opinions unless you're a physician. And don't selectively omit information. If you have breathing or bleeding problems, indicate these first, firmly and clearly. *Reason:* Life-threatening conditions are given priority.

After seeing the triage nurse—and sometimes even before—you must make arrangements for payment. *Helpful:* On your medical-history card, include information about your medical-insurance coverage, date of birth, Social Security number, and the name, address, and phone number of your employer. *Warning:* At some hospitals you may be turned away if you can't arrange for payment.

For complex conditions: Go to a large teaching hospital. *Advantage:* University affiliation...best-trained staff...advanced technology that most other hospitals can't afford to provide.

Hospitals in general, including teaching hospitals, come in three varieties: Private for-profit, private not-for-profit, and government-run public hospitals. *Myth:* Public hospitals are the worst...some are, in fact, excellent.

Advantage of for-profit hospitals: They're usually less crowded because they generally turn away people who can't pay. Private not-for-profit hospitals, many of which receive funding that obligates them to serve the indigent, and public hospitals tend to be crowded. If you're a high-priority case and your public hospital is a teaching hospital, you may get the best care there.

Important: Location of a hospital...and contracts that it may have to care for special groups. Hospitals that receive admissions from "combat zones" or are convenient to transportation are likely to have a crowded emergency room. Hospitals that have a contract to treat emergency cases from a local mental hospital, center for the retarded, prison, or shelter are also apt to be more crowded...often with high-priority cases. A low-priority case, such as a broken arm, might be treated faster at a walk-in emergency medical center—where it would be a high priority.

Hospitals that take Medicaid and Medicare (almost all) are always more crowded in areas where few doctors accept these types of insurance. *Reason:* People simply go to the ER in lieu of a doctor's office. Especially crowded time in all ERs: Saturday nights.

Inside information:

If you arrive at a hospital by ambulance, you will generally receive a higher priority...even if you could have gotten to the hospital without the ambulance. If your condition is serious enough to warrant that taking an ambulance isn't frivolous, it's a good strategy to call one. *Best:* Arriving in the hospital's own ambulance, because you automatically become one of its patients...and its patients receive priority.

For the same reason, the ambulance of a local volunteer unit or fire district is a good choice. These people know the local ER personnel, and they are your neighbors. *Recommended:* Contribute to their fund drives and post your contribution stickers. *If your condition is very serious:* Call the police—always dial 911. Police response with an ambulance—or transport by the police themselves, if no ambulance is available—will facilitate matters at the hospital. *Helpful:* Call the ambulance a *bus*—the inside term used by police. *Aim:* To get them to assume that you or a close relative is a cop and render service accordingly.

Source: Harry Alberts, MSW, certified social worker, Box 402, Commack, NY 11725, 718-353-HELP. Mr. Alberts was formerly with the New York State Department of Health.

Alcohol Without Hangovers

Some hangover discomfort is caused by *congeners* (toxic chemicals formed during fermentation). Vodka has the lowest congener content, gin next. Blended scotch has four times the congener content of gin. Brandy, rum, and pure malt scotch have six times that amount, bourbon eight times.

Retard the absorption of alcohol by eating before and during drinking (especially foods, such as cheese, that contain fatty proteins).

Use tap water as a mixer. Carbonation speeds the absorption of alcohol.

If you get a hangover anyway, the only known cures are rest, aspirin, and time. The endless roster of other remedies—ranging from cucumber juice and salt to a Bloody Mary—have more to do with drinking mythology than with medical fact, although according to psychologists who have studied hangovers, if you believe in a cure, it may help.

When Blood Pressure Can Fool You

Blood-pressure readings are often deceptively high when taken in a hospital or a doctor's office. *Reason:* The patient's system reacts to anxiety over the test or to the doctor's presence. In an Italian study, 47 of 48 patients' pressure rose after the doctor appeared. (In one case, the systolic reading went up 75 points.) *Solution:* When three or four measurements were taken over a period of 10 minutes, the last was likely to be accurate.

Source: *New Scientist*, King's Reach Tower, Stamford St., London SE1 9LS.

Collecting More on Your Company Health Policy

Health insurance policies are not etched in stone. There are contractual provisions in the insurance policy that are negotiable.

Most companies give health insurance to engender goodwill among employees. Many problems in collecting the maximum due you are a result of incompetence or negligence on the part of the administrators in your company who handle insurance benefits. They may be too busy or unaware of how to get more for you.

Three ways to improve your ability to collect:

• Know the insurance contract and all its provisions. Be aware that everything is negotiable. *Example:* Home health care by someone other than a registered or practical nurse is not covered in the policy. Contractually, nothing needs to be said, but administratively, an alternate source of home health care could be covered. It is really a question of negotiation.

• Have the company's insurance broker help negotiate with the insurer. He/she is the one who is making the money from selling your company the policy. He also has more leverage than you do with the insurance company. If he is unwilling to help, encourage your company to switch to a more cooperative broker.

• Set up a liaison. The individual in your company in charge of claims should have a good working relationship with the insurance company. *Reason:* If the settlement is too low or doesn't fully cover your needs, the claims person at your firm can make a better settlement. After all, the insurance company is selling the policies.

Strategy: If your claims person is uncertain whether you can get more compensation for an ailment or treatment, ask for permission to contact the broker. The broker should know the terms of your contract and be familiar with the people at the insurance company. He should have an idea of how to get the claim paid, especially if it's a legitimate claim but a trifle unusual.

Take advantage of situations in which both you and your spouse are covered by group insurance policies to increase your benefits.

Example: You both have Blue Cross to cover hospitalization and, in addition, you both have major medical. Typically, the major medical has a $100 deductible. The insurance company will pick up 80% of the next $2,000 and 100% thereafter. However, if you and your spouse coordinate your policies, you could wind up using each other's policy to pay the remaining 20% of the $2,000.

Don't expect to make a profit by having several insurance policies. Years ago, many health insurance policies were not coordinated and it was possible to get duplicate payments. Today all plans are coordinated so you *can't* get duplicate payments.

Trying to make specifically unallowable treatments allowable: This is between the doctor and you. For instance, if you want to claim cosmetic surgery necessary for health reasons, consult your doctor. If he won't go along with it, you are not going to get anywhere with the insurance broker, the personnel at your office, or the insurance company.

If you are stuck with a flawed company policy and find you have huge deductibles and other uncovered expenses, take out a personal policy that coordinates with the company's.

Source: Leonard Stern, president, Leonard B. Stern & Co., an insurance consulting and brokerage firm, 65 E. 55 St., Suite 303, New York 10022.

How to Find a Good Nursing Home

Most families postpone the decision to use a nursing home for as long as possible. Once the decision is reached, the process of selecting a good facility is so painful that often they move too fast. *Good advice:* Give the parent involved time to get used to the idea. Meanwhile, investigate every possible choice thoroughly.

How to begin: Get lists of not-for-profit, community-based homes from your church, fraternal order, state agency on aging, the American Association of Homes for the Aging (Suite 770, 1050 17th St. NW, Washington, DC 20036), or the American Health Care Association (1200 15th St. NW, Washington, DC 20005).

Costs: If parents' resources are small, Medicaid may provide financial support for nursing-home care. Homes offering complete care in metropolitan areas usually charge $50–$80 per day (depending on the amount of care required). Some require a large advance gift or admission fee. (Health insurance sometimes covers nursing homes.) Patients who pay their own way may be eligible for Medicaid assistance after their savings run out. Check the rules in your state.

Evaluating a Nursing Home

1. Accreditation, license, and certification for Medicare and Medicaid should be current and in force.

2. *Best to arrive without an appointment.* Look at everything. The building and rooms should be clean, attractive, safe, and meet all fire codes. Residents should not be crowded (ask about private rooms; sometimes they're available at reasonable extra cost). Visit the dining room at mealtime. Check the kitchen, too. Visit activity rooms when in session. Talk to residents to find out how they feel about the home.

3. The staff should be professionally trained and large enough to provide adequate care for all residents.

4. *If the home requires a contract, read it carefully.* Show it to your lawyer before signing. Some homes reserve the right to discharge patients whose condition has deteriorated, even if a lump-sum payment was made upon admittance. *Best:* An agreement that allows payment by the month or permits refunds or advance payment if circumstances change.

5. Find out exactly what services the home provides and which ones cost extra. Private-duty nurses are not included. Such extras as shampoo and hair set can be exorbitant. (A box of tissue can cost a dollar.) Make a list of the "extras" your parent will need for a comfortable life. Try to supply some of them yourself.

Before you decide on a home, you and your parent should have a talk with the administrator and department heads. Find out who is in charge of what, and whom to speak to if problems arise.

Source: Sheldon Goldberg, Am. Ass'n. of Homes for the Aging.

Nonstick Pan Alert

Nonstick pans (such as Teflon or Silverstone) can be dangerous if allowed to boil dry. At 400°F, the pans may release toxic fumes after 20 minutes—enough to make a person sick. *Especially susceptible:* birds and other pets.

Alternative Medicine: How to Cure a Cold

Recent research has shown that a technique called *visualization* is effective in curing colds by strengthening the body's immune system.

Basic idea: Every morning and evening for 15 minutes and every hour for 2 to 5 minutes, relax and visualize yourself getting well.

To relax: Slow your breathing (take deeper breaths). Direct your attention inward by following your breath to the center of your body. Enter a peaceful state of picturing a ball of golden light.

To visualize: Keep it simple. See yourself well, with a clear, uncongested nose, throat, and chest.

Imagine the cells in the distressed area of your body being cleaned by luminous white cells.

Source: Barbara A. Brennan, an experienced psychic healer and bioenergetic therapist, is president, Healing Science Institute, 331 E. 71 St., Box 21, New York 10021. The institute offers a four-year training program in healing.

Cordless Phone Alert

Cordless phones have caused partial hearing loss in several users. The problem is that the phone's ringer is located within the earpiece and can ring in the ear at sound levels of up to 141 decibels. *Solution:* Don't forget to flip the switch from *standby* to *talk* every time the phone is answered.

How to Change Your Biological Age

Gray hair, wrinkled skin, growing flabbiness, loss of vitality and reduced resistance to injury and disease...

To most Americans, these are harbingers of old age, unwelcome but inevitable milestones along a path that leads inexorably to the grave. In fact, recent research suggests something quite different—that the body's gradual decline stems not from the passing of years but from the combined effects of inactivity and poor nutrition. So no matter what your present health status or your chronological age—regular exercise—and improved eating habits will lower your biological age.

Benefits: Reduced body fat...increased muscle mass...strength increases of 200% to 300%... increases in aerobic capacity by 20% or more... and reduced risk of heart disease, diabetes, osteoporosis and other age-related ailments.

Your goal should not be to become immortal, but to remain healthy and vigorous for as long as possible...and to compress the inevitable period of decline preceding death from several years into a few weeks or months.

To gauge your biological age: Forget how many birthdays you've marked...instead consider how you stack up in terms of the 10 key "biomarkers" identified by our lab...

•Muscle mass. As Americans move from adolescence into old age, we lose almost seven pounds of lean body mass each decade—a rate that accelerates after age 45.

Reduced muscle mass leads not only to reduced strength, but also to an increased risk of heart disease and diabetes, reduced aerobic capacity and a slower metabolism (which promotes gain of fat). All because of bad habits like driving instead of walking or riding a bike, taking elevators rather than stairs...and because we're all too willing to let younger friends and relatives do chores we should do ourselves.

Good news: Those who remain physically active lose little muscle tissue as they age. All it takes is 20 to 30 minutes of aerobic exercise two or three times weekly.

•Strength. Between the ages of 20 and 70, the average American loses about 30% of his muscle cells—including a large proportion of "fast-twitch" cells needed for sprinting and other high-exertion exercise.

Unchecked, this loss of muscle leads eventually to sarcopenia, the severe, debilitating weakness that makes independent living impossible.

Good news: While we cannot prevent loss of muscle cells, a weight-lifting regimen will compensate by boosting the size and strength of the cells that remain.

Essential: Ten repetitions of 10 lifts with a weight that should leave your muscles completely fatigued. If not, add more weight.

•Metabolic rate. Because more energy is needed to maintain muscle than fat, the less muscle tissue in your body, the slower your metabolism—and the fewer calories you must consume to maintain ideal body weight. Beginning at age 20, the average person's metabolic rate drops about 2% per decade. Thus the average 70-year-old needs 500 fewer calories a day than the average 25-year-old.

Problem: Many middle-aged Americans continue eating as if they were 20. *Eventual result:* Obesity. To fight fat, eat fewer calories and get enough exercise to maintain your muscle mass.

•Body fat percentage. In most cases, advancing age brings not only muscle loss but fat gain. Even if our weight (as measured by a scale) changes little, the ratio of fat to lean in our bodies can rise markedly over the years.

The body of the average 25-year-old woman is 25% fat, for example, while the average 65-year-old woman is about 43% fat.

For men, the numbers rise from 18% fat at age 25 to 38% at 65.

Danger: Excessive fat leads to chronic disease and premature death.

Especially dangerous: Fat around the waist. It's far more unhealthy than fat on the buttocks or thighs.

To lose fat and gain muscle: Combine a low-fat diet with regular exercise.

•Aerobic capacity. To gauge fitness, doctors often measure the body's ability to process oxygen during exercise. The greater this aerobic capacity, the faster oxygen is pumped throughout the body—and the fitter the individual. Like other biomarkers, aerobic capacity often declines with age. Typically, by age 65 it is 30% to 40% below its level in young adulthood.

Good news: Regular, aerobic exercise—the kind that causes huffing and puffing—will raise your aerobic capacity no matter what your present age. The longer and harder your workouts, the greater the benefit.

•Blood-sugar tolerance. For most Americans, aging brings about a gradual decline in the body's ability to metabolize blood sugar (glucose). So common is this problem that by age 70—20% of men and 30% of women are at increased risk of diabetes, a potential killer.

At special risk for problems: The overweight, the sedentary and those who eat a fatty diet.

Good news: A low-fat, high-fiber diet, combined with regular exercise, will cut your diabetes risk. Be sure to include both strength- building and aerobic exercise in your routine.

•Cholesterol ratio. As most of us already know, a high cholesterol level boosts your risk of heart disease. But total cholesterol isn't the only thing that counts.

Very important: The ratio of total cholesterol to HDL (good) cholesterol. For older people, the ideal ratio is 4.5 or lower. A person whose total cholesterol is 200 and whose HDL is 50, for example, has a ratio of 200/50, or 4.0.

To lower your ratio: Stop smoking, lose weight, reduce your intake of fatty, cholesterol-rich foods (especially animal products) and exercise regularly. Exercise is the only way to boost HDL levels.

•Blood pressure. In many parts of the world, advancing age brings little if any change in blood pressure. In the US, however, where older people tend to be both overweight and sedentary, blood pressure does rise with age, often spiralling far above the maximum "safe" level of 145/80.

To keep pressure in check: Stay slim, don't smoke, get regular exercise and limit your consumption of fat, salt and alcohol. If these steps fail, pressure-lowering drugs may be necessary.

•Bone density. As we age, our skeletons slowly become weaker and more brittle. While some mineral loss is inevitable, the severe and potentially deadly condition known as osteoporosis is not.

Prevention: Although consuming at least 800 milligrams of calcium a day will retard the loss of bone, that alone rarely does the trick. *Also needed:* Weight-bearing exercise, such as walking, running or cycling.

Not helpful: Swimming and other forms of exercise that do not subject the long bones to the stress of gravity.

Source: William J. Evans, PhD, chief of the human physiology lab at the Human Nutrition Research Center on Aging, a Boston-based facility operated jointly by the US Department of Agriculture and Tufts University. Dr. Evans is the coauthor of *Biomarkers: The 10 Keys for Prolonging Vitality.* Fireside Books, 1230 Avenue of the Americas, New York 10020.

How To Be Less Lonely...

While little careful research has been done on the effectiveness of interventions for loneliness—there are some promising strategies...

•Cognitive therapy. Exploring and challenging the negative assumptions of lonely people might encourage them to take social risks...and make them more attractive to others.

•Social skills practice. Some university counseling centers and community mental health clinics offer group workshops on overcoming shyness. Role-playing and other methods can help lonely people build confidence and learn to interact more successfully with others.

•Changing the environment. Many people have trouble forming relationships not because of any deficit in social skills, but because they're not spending time in the right places.

Example: Loneliness is a common reaction to moving to a new city. Work is the basis for many people's social lives. If you have little in common with your colleagues other than the fact that you work together, you'll be at a disadvantage in finding people to socialize with.

In fact, it can be dangerous to overemphasize a lack of personal and social skills as a cause of loneliness. Studies have shown that people who focus on their situations—and try to do something to change their situations—are more successful at overcoming loneliness than people who blame their own presumed personality defects.

Successful relationships are largely a function of *proximity and similarity*...being in settings where you are likely to meet people who share your interests, education level, socioeconomic background, age or hobbies.

Example: Trying to meet people of the opposite sex in bars, or even many singles groups, is highly unlikely to result in *satisfying* long-term relationships. The people you meet there may be pleasant, but the odds are you'll have nothing in common with them...and the future of such relationships is not promising.

Think about what you are interested in and where people with the same interests as yourself are likely to be found—then go there. People too often overlook this seemingly obvious but effective strategy.

Source: Daniel Russell, PhD, a social psychologist and associate professor in the College of Medicine at the University of Iowa. With psychologists L. Ann Peplau and Carolyn Cutrona, he developed the UCLA Loneliness Scale, which has become a standard instrument used by psychologists to measure loneliness.

Investment

Key Questions to Ask When Selecting a Stockbroker

Be sure that *you* do the interviewing. Don't let the prospective broker turn the tables and interview you. Here are some key areas to cover when interviewing a potential stockbroker:

•Where and what did he/she study?

•How long has he been with the brokerage firm? How long has he been in the securities industry? What was his prior employment? Why did he leave his last place of employment?

•Where does he get his investment recommendations? His firm's research department? Company contacts? Friends in the business? His own research? A combination?

•Can he supply a certified history of his firm's and his own research recommendations?

•Does he have any client references?

•What is his theory on giving sell advice and profit taking?

•How many clients does the account executive service? (You want your telephone calls to be answered promptly.)

•How diversified is the brokerage firm? Does it have, for example, a bond department? How about an economist? An in-house market technician (essential for timing)? Money-market experts? Commodities department? Option department? Tax-shelter experts?

•How many industries does the firm's research department follow? How many companies? How many senior analysts does the firm have?

•Will you be getting weekly, monthly, or only occasional printed research reports?

•What fees, if any, will be charged for such services as securities safekeeping?

•What is the firm's commission structure? What discounts is it willing to offer?

•Can the investor talk directly to the investment-research analyst to get firsthand clarifications and updates on research reports? Must everything be funneled through the account executive?

•What is the financial condition of the brokerage firm? (You'll want to see the latest annual and quarterly financial statements.)

•How many floor brokers does the firm have at the various stock exchanges? (You'll want prompt order execution.)

•Is the potential broker willing to meet personally on a regular basis (monthly or quarterly, depending on portfolio size and activity) to discuss progress?

•What kind of monthly customer statements are prepared? (More and more firms now offer tabulation of monthly dividend income, portfolio valuation, and annual portfolio yield estimate for their customers.)

The Scandalous Wall Street "Specials"

One of the more insidious stockbroker-dealer practices is the use of specials to dispose of inventory. When a brokerage firm wants to dump an over-the-counter (unlisted) security that it has in its own inventory, it substantially increases the commission it pays to its account executives if they sell it promptly.

Since the security comes out of the firm's inventory, the transaction is called a principal transaction. These are generally done on a net basis. On the confirmation slip the customer receives, there is no breakdown between the actual price of the security and the commission charged. *Result:* The customer doesn't really know the exact commission or the stock's precise price. This obfuscation allows the broker to charge a higher price for the security than may be dictated by supply and demand. As a result of this ploy, the firm can afford to give its account executives the higher commissions.

Why is the account executive so eager to sell you a particular security? Does it really fit into your investment program? Does he have a research report recommending it?

There are two main reasons brokers want to unload stocks in their inventory. They have become disenchanted with the stock's prospects, or the carrying (interest) charges have become excessive. Some firms announce "specials" to the account executives on an almost daily basis.

Safeguard: One of the most important safeguards any investor should employ is to ask his/her account executive for a research report on any recommendation that is made, even if it is only a brief one.

Confirmation slips should indicate when a brokerage firm is selling stock out of its own inventory by stating that it is a principal transaction. Some brokers, however, merely indicate that the transaction was done on a net basis and that the firm is a "market maker." An investor who sees these terms may have been an unwitting purchaser of a "special" that was sold to him only because his account executive was eager to get a higher commission. In order to mislead clients, some brokerage firms merely put a small code number on the front of the confirmation slip. On the back of that slip, in tiny print, you will find that the code number means that, in fact, a principal transaction was done.

Bottom line: Instruct your broker to inform you beforehand whether the transaction is likely to be a principal or an agency transaction, which means that the broker is acting as a middleman or on behalf of another investor. Confirmation slips for agency transactions should state separate price and commission charges.

How to Earn Interest in Two Money-Market Funds On the Same Money

Squeeze out a little bit more income by playing the float.

Switch money from one fund to another. Although deposits are credited almost immediately, it takes a few days for money-fund checks to clear. That means an investor can legally earn daily interest in two places from the same money.

One Florida resident keeps $10,000 in five different funds. Each month he mails a $5,000 check from one fund to another, trying to ensure that his deposits arrive on a Thursday. He is credited by Friday, but that money won't come out of his other fund until Tuesday. Meanwhile, for five days he appears to have $15,000 in each account.

There are variations on this strategy, such as switching money from NOW accounts into money-market funds. If the NOW account is in a savings and loan institution (these are outside the Federal Reserve System), it takes even longer for that deposit to clear. Other investors have used money-fund checks to buy Treasury bills. Again, they earn double interest for a few days.

Floating between funds may seem like more of a headache than it's worth. Still, there are simple ways to maximize your money-market dividends, such as paying all bills, including the IRS's, with money-fund checks.

Funds require a $500 minimum on withdrawals. If your total monthly expenses add up to only $500, write checks from your regular checking account and then transfer money from your fund at the last possible moment to cover those disbursements. It's foolish to keep much in a checking account these days.

Some funds seem to be encouraging investors to play the float by offering check-writing privileges on distant banks. Sending checks drawn from West Coast banks to East Cost creditors is nothing new. Businesses have been doing so for many years. Now consumers can play the same game and earn interest in the bargain.

When to Sell a Stock

It's very difficult to know when to sell a stock. Very little research has been done on the subject, and advice from brokers is usually vague and confusing. *Typical comments:* "Let's watch it one more day." "Can't sell it now, but you should get out on the next rally." "It's not doing well right now, but it's sure to come back over the long haul." If the stock you've bought has gone up, the two conflicting clichés on Wall Street are: "Can't get hurt taking a profit" and "Let your profits run."

What to do instead: When it comes to evaluating an individual stock, you should look for one thing—failure. This sounds austere, but what to look for is very specific: A stock that tries to rally and fails to make a new high.

How to identify failure: The stock must sell *below* the price level at which it had held in a previous "correction" (decline). If you were to look at this sequence on a stock chart, you would see a series of lower highs and lower lows. That type of action establishes failure. It defines the stock's trend as down, not up.

Sell! Put aside all hopes that the stock will stabilize or rally wildly, or that it will come back if you hold it long enough. The market is telling you, in no uncertain terms, that something is wrong. You don't have to know what or why. That information frequently doesn't come out until the stock has tumbled a very long distance. You've made an objective decision. Stick with it.

When to decide to sell: When the stock market is closed. That way, each little gyration won't affect your decision emotionally.

After you've made an objective decision, use a protective stop order. *How it works:* Tell your broker to sell the stock automatically when it drops below a certain point.

You can use stop orders effectively, even if the

stock rises. Each time the price advances, cancel the old stop order and enter a new one. *One arbitrary rule:* Set the stop order price at 10% below the current stock market price.

Source: *When to Sell*, by Justin Mamis and Robert Mamis, Farrar, Straus & Giroux, 19 Union Sq. West, New York 10003.

How Options Traders Make Money in a Declining Market

Now that trading in listed *puts* is available on five option exchanges, let's see how to use them.

*Puts** provide a way of selling stock short in hopes of a market decline, without the risk of severe loss usually associated with short selling.

How puts work: Suppose XYZ Corp. is selling at $50 and you can purchase a January-50 *put* on the options exchange for $350. The *put* entitles you to sell 100 shares of XYZ at 50 until the expiration of that option.

If XYZ were to decline to, say, 40, an option carrying the right to sell the shares at 50 would be worth $1,000 (the $10 difference times 100 shares). The profit would accrue immediately to the option holder, who could exercise the option on shares that he/she could purchase on the open market at 40. Even better, since the commissions would be lower, he could simply sell the option for $1,000. Since he paid $350, his gain would be $650, or 186%, on a stock that declined 20%.

Of course, if XYZ rose or stood still through the life of the option, the option would expire. This would result in a 100% loss. However, the maximum risk to the short-seller using the *put* would be $350, the cost of the option.

Straddles: More Flexibility

The availability of listed *puts*, used with *call*† options, provides some interesting opportunities for mathematically oriented investors. *Straddles (using puts and calls) can produce profit regardless of the direction of the market movement, provided the underlying common stock moves away from its starting price by a certain amount.*

Example:

Assume XYZ is at 50 again, the listed *put* selling for $350 ($3^1/_2$) and the listed January *call*, which entitles the option holder to *buy 100* shares at 50, also selling at $3^1/_2$. Instead of purchasing the *put* alone, you purchase *both*. Here are the workouts at different prices of XYZ when both options expire on a given date.

**Put:* The right to sell shares of a specified price until a specified date.
†*Call:* The right to buy a specified stock at a specified price until a specified date.

Price XYZ	Put Value	Gain (Loss)	Call Value	Gain (Loss)	Net
70	0	-350	20	+1650	+1300
65	0	-350	15	+1150	+800
60	0	-350	10	+650	+300
55	0	-350	5	+150	-200
50	0	-350	0	-350	-700
45	5	+150	0	-350	-200
40	10	+650	0	-350	+300
35	15	+1150	0	-350	+800
30	20	+1650	0	-350	+1300

The position shows a profit as long as XYZ moves beyond the 43–57 price range, a 14% movement in either direction from the starting price of 50.

It's possible to profit on both sides of a straddle. *Example:* If XYZ first rises to 60 and then falls to 40, *you might sell or exercise your call at a profit in the rise and then sell or exercise your put for an additional profit in the fall.* However, in practice, one or the other side of a straddle is usually exercised, not both.

Straddles are best purchased after the market has rested within a trading range for some time and you expect a breakout but are uncertain of the direction. And, of course, you should purchase an option only when option premiums (the price of options) are running below normal.

Techniques for Evaluating Over-the-Counter Stocks

Growth potential is the single most important consideration. Earnings increases should average 10% over the past six years when acquisitions and divestitures are factored out. Cash, investments, accounts receivable, materials, and inventories should be twice the size of financial claims due within the next year.

In addition, working capital per share should be greater than the market value of the stock (an $8 stock should be backed by $10 per share in working capital). Long-term debt should be covered by working capital, cash, or one year's income. And the balance sheet should show no deferred operating expenses and no unreceived income.

The criteria for final selections include ownership by at least 10 institutions reported in *Standard & Poor's Stock Guide* and public ownership of between 500,000 and 1 million shares, with no more than 10% controlled by a single institution. There should also be continued price increases after a dividend or split, and a strong likelihood of moving up to a major exchange (a good sign of strong broker and institutional support).

OTC stocks to avoid are those of companies that are expanding into unrelated fields, where they lack the required management experience and depth, and stocks selling at prices far below recent highs. This sign of loss of investor support can take months to overcome.

Source: C. Colburn Hardy, *Physician's Management*, New York.

A Guide to Market Indicators

•*The speculation index.* Divide the weekly trading volume on the American Stock Exchange (in thousands) by the number of issues traded. Calculate the same ratio for New York Stock Exchange trading. Divide the AMEX ratio by the NYSE ratio to calculate the speculation index. Strategists believe the market is bearish when the index is more than .38 (and especially so if it rises to .38 and then falls back). Less than .20 is bullish.

•*Member short selling.* Divide the number of shares NYSE members sell short each week by the total NYSE short selling. The index is bearish when readings of .87 are reached. A reading below .75 is very bullish, particularly if it lasts several weeks.

•*New highs—new lows.* The market is usually approaching an intermediate bottom when the number of new lows reaches 600. The probable sign of an intermediate top is 600 new highs in one week, followed by a decline in number the next week.

•*The NYSE short-interest ratio.* The total number of outstanding shares sold short each month divided by the average daily trading volume for that month. A strong rally generally comes after the ratio reaches 1.75.

•*The 10-week moving NYSE average.* Compute the average NYSE index for the previous 10 weeks, then measure the difference between last week's close and the average. When the gap between the last weekly close and the 10-week average remains at 4.0 or below for two or three weeks, investors can expect an intermediate advance. Market tops are usually near when the last week's index is 4.0 or more above the previous 10-week average.

Only once or twice a year will as many as four of the five indicators signal an intermediate bottom. But when four do, it is highly reliable. The same is true for intermediate tops.

Source: *Barron's*, New York, and *Indicator Digest*, Palisades Park, NJ.

How to Get Reimbursed for Past Stock Market Losses

Investors who have lost money in the stock market through the negligence, misrepresentation, or manipulation of a broker have a better than 50% chance of recouping those funds through an arbitration process mandated by the U.S. Supreme Court in 1987.

Grounds for complaint:

•Unsuitable investments (putting a modest retirement fund into risky stocks, options or limited partnerships, for example).

•Misrepresentation (failing to disclose an investment's risk when recommending it).

•Churning (trading your account excessively to run up brokerage fees).

•Unauthorized trading (buying and selling without your permission).

•Failing to obey (not executing your trade order in a timely fashion).

How to fight back: First, carefully check confirmation slips as soon as you receive them and reconcile them with your monthly statement. As soon as you see that something is wrong, notify your broker's branch manager of your complaint in writing, with copies to the broker and the firm's compliance department. Don't call your broker direct—you put him/her on guard to cover mistakes. This first letter may be enough to make the firm settle to your satisfaction.

If the brokerage firm won't make good your loss, you will have to proceed into arbitration. Look at your contract with the brokerage house. It probably requires you to take your case to one of the industry's 10 self-regulatory organizations (SROs). Sponsored by the National Association of Stock Dealers or the New York Stock Exchange, SROs have become fairer to the public since 1989 (by law two nonindustry arbitors must now be included on every three-person panel) and their filing fees start at $15. The alternative to SROs is the American Arbitration Association (AAA), which requires higher fees ($300—and up).

What are your odds? The appointment of more arbitors from outside the industry and new discovery rules, which allow you greater access to the brokerage company's records before the hearing, are giving investors a better chance to get justice. In 1991, investors won awards from SRO arbitors in 51.3% of the cases. The figure for 1990 was 53.4%. In 1991, AAA panels granted awards to investors in 60% of the cases. The awards made by AAA panels were proportionately higher, but both arbitor organizations have awarded court costs and punitive damages.

Do you need a lawyer? Few lawyers will take a case involving less than $25,000 on a contingency fee. However, you can effectively present your own case if you hire a lawyer to advise you on how to proceed, how to obtain the documentation you need, and even, if you want it, to ghostwrite your claim.

For cases involving more than $25,000, you should hire a lawyer to evaluate your claim and represent you at the arbitration hearing.

Buy a Business—With No Money Down

Common dilemma: The owner of a company—call him Mr. Brown—is 65 years old and wants to sell his business. The person best qualified to continue running it (so the company will command a high price) is the general manager—call him Mr. Jones. Jones would like to own the company, but he lacks the cash to buy it.

One solution might be for Jones to try to set up a leveraged buyout. But there are drawbacks:

- The venture will be burdened by collateralized bank loans at high interest rates.
- With heavy loan exposure, banks may be tempted to interfere in the management of the business.
- If Jones has no cash at all, he could wind up with little equity in the company.

From Brown's point of view, the other familiar route to sell his company is through a public offering.

The drawbacks:

- The 1987 stock market crash has made it difficult to raise money by public offerings.
- The red tape of the Securities & Exchange Commission is enormous. Ironically, there are even more SEC restrictions for an established business that wants to go public than there are to start a new business.

New financing options:

Individuals eager to invest in promising companies have set up blind pools. The pools are simply investment funds structured so that the pool takes an equity position in ventures it finances, but members take no management responsibility in the businesses they buy.

Blind pools have been around for a long time, especially in western mining states. Now they're more popular than ever.

How blind pools work:

Brown wants to sell his XYZ Co. to Jones, the general manager, for $2 million. In a typical deal, Brown would guarantee a $100,000 bank loan for Jones so he can afford a down payment. Brown also signs a letter giving Jones an option to buy the company for $2 million.

Jones takes the letter to a blind pool, which has $200,000 cash and whose stock is traded on the over-the-counter market. If pool management believes the company has a good chance of continued growth and profitability, it can agree to acquire it at that point.

When that happens, they issue new stock in the blind pool so that 85% of the total of the pool is owned by Jones—with 15% ownership remaining with the pool. As part of the transaction, Jones assigns to the pool his right to buy Brown's company.

The $100,000 down payment to Brown comes from the pool. The rest of the payments made to Brown come from the company's subsequent cash flow and are secured by Jones's stock in the pool.

Moreover, the additional $100,000 that the pool originally had is now available to the company to spend on growth.

What the main players get:

- Brown gets to sell his business at the price he wants to a person he knows can run it. He also gets a stream of payments during his retirement years. He may also receive shares and options for shares in the pool, as well as possible consulting agreements.
- Jones gets 85% of the company without using any of his own money.
- Pool members acquire a company that's worth at least $2 million.

The best way to find blind pools is through lawyers, accountants, or brokers who specialize in venture capital and securities matters. If you don't know a professional in one of these fields, ask your own accountant or attorney. He/she can probably put you in touch with one.

Stay away from a blind pool if:

- One or more of its members suggest a side deal, either with the buyer or the seller. It's a sign of shady operating.
- There is discussion about the stock, which implies manipulation that violates SEC law.

Source: Dan Brecher, head of the investment banking department, Bower & Gardner, 110 E. 59 St., New York 10022.

Making Profits on a Stock Split

When a stock splits, the average profit to an investor is 20%. But the greatest profits are generally made in three to six months before the split is announced. The general pattern is that the price stays high for two days after the split announcement and then declines.

To spot a candidate for a split, look for:

- A company that needs to attract more stockholders, diversify, or attract additional financing.

•A takeover candidate (heavy in cash and liquid assets) whose management holds only a small percentage of the outstanding shares. (Companies with concentrated ownership rarely split stock unless there are problems with taxes, acquisitions, or diversification.)

•A stock priced above $75. A split moves it into the more attractive $25–$50 range.

•A stock that was split previously whose price has climbed steadily since then.

•Earnings prospects so strong that the company will be able to increase dividends after the split.

Attractive prospects are over-the-counter companies with current earnings of $2.5 million, at least $2 million annually in preceding years and less than 1 million shares outstanding (or under 2,000 shareholders). A stock split is necessary if management wants to list on a major exchange.

Source: C. Colburn Hardy, *Dun & Bradstreet's Guide to Investments*, Thomas Y. Crowell Co., New York.

Spotting Low-Priced Stocks Ready to Bounce Back

The key to success in the stock market is knowing how to recognize value. Here is the successful approach of Robert Ravitz, director of research at the investment management firm David J. Greene & Co.

At the Greene operation, value has little to do with a good versus a bad company. A top-quality large company selling at a high price/earnings multiple is less attractive than a lesser-quality company selling at a depressed price in terms of its past and future earning power, working capital, book value, and historical prices.

Here is where Greene's analysts look for value:

Stocks that have just made a new low for the past 12 months.

Companies that are likely to be liquidated. In the process of liquidation, shareholders may get paid considerably more than the stock is selling for now.

Unsuccessful merger candidates. If one buyer thinks a company's stock is a good value, it's possible that others may also come to the same conclusion.

Companies that have just reduced or eliminated their dividends. The stock is usually hit with a selling wave, which often creates a good buying opportunity.

Financially troubled companies in which another major company has a sizable ownership position. If the financial stake is large enough, you can be sure that the major company will do everything it can to turn the earnings around and get the stock price up so that its investment will work out.

Opportunities, also, in stocks that are totally washed out—that is, situations where all the bad news is out. The stock usually has nowhere to go but up.

How to be sure a stock is truly washed out:

Trading volume slows to practically nothing.

No Wall Street research analysts are following the company anymore.

No financial journalists, stock market newsletters, or advisory services discuss the company.

Selling of the stock by the company's management and directors has stopped.

Signs of a turnabout:

The company plans to get rid of a losing division or business. If so, be sure to learn whether the company will be able to report a big jump in earnings once the losing operation is sold.

The company is selling off assets to improve its financial situation and/or reduce debt.

A new management comes on board with an established track record of success with turnaround situations.

Management begins buying the company's stock in the open market.

Also, be sure to follow 13d statements filed with the Securities and Exchange Commission (SEC). A company or individual owning 5% or more of a public company must report such holdings to the SEC. If any substantial company is acquiring a major position in a company, it's possible that a tender offer at a much higher price is in the wind.

Source: Robert Ravitz, director of research, David J. Greene & Co., an investment management firm, 30 Wall St., New York 10005.

Travel

New Tricks for the Shrewd Traveler

Getting the seat you prefer on an airplane has become increasingly difficult. Reaching the airport at a reasonable time before takeoff used to ensure a decent seat. But this is no longer the case, since airlines preassign seats when reservations are made.

Best Strategies

If you're assigned to a seat you don't like, go back to the desk when all the prereserved seats are released (usually 15 minutes before flight time). All the prime seats for passengers who didn't show up are available then.

If on the plane you discover that you don't like your seat, don't wait until the plane takes off to find a better one. Look around the plane, and the second before they close the door, head for the empty seat of your choice. Don't wait until the seat-belt sign goes on.

By prereserving a single seat on a nonjumbo where the seats are three across, you'll increase the odds of getting an empty seat next to you. Ask for a window or aisle seat in a row where the window or aisle is already reserved by a *single.* The middle seat between two singles is least likely to fill up. *Desperation measure:* Say you're very overweight and need an empty seat next to you so you won't crowd the other passengers.

Flight Tactics

There are other facts that every shrewd traveler should know:

•If you carry a hanging bag on the plane and put it in one of those little front closets, someone else can easily take it by mistake. Those bags all look alike. *Be aware:* Luggage you carry onto the plane *is not insured* against such mishaps. *Remedy:* Tie a bright-colored ribbon or string around the handle. A name tag isn't enough. If someone else picks up your bag, the ribbon should alert him/her to the mistake.

•If you change your reservation to a different flight and your ticket must be changed, don't wait in the long line at the airline's front desk. As long as your destination remains the same, you can take your ticket directly to the gate and change it there—even if you've switched airlines or fares. The desk at the gate has a charge card imprinter to deal with any changes. *Added advantage:* You're less likely to miss your flight by waiting in line if you're already at the gate.

•If you've rented a car and don't want to drag your bags on and off the rental agency's airport bus, drop your bags off *first* at the curbside check-in and *then* return the car. *Tip the curbside checker.* You don't want your luggage to be "accidentally" misrouted. Advise the attending porter of your destination.

Handling Hotels

When you arrive at the hotel, check your bags. Then go to the pay telephone in the lobby and call the hotel. Ask to have your reservation confirmed, give them your charge-card number, and go on your way. *Reason:* You'll sidestep convention check-in lines.

To avoid the long line after the convention, go down to the desk very early in the morning, before official checkout time, and check out. You won't have to turn in your room key, and you can still use your room until official checkout time (usually around 1 P.M.).

Don't stay in your hotel room if you're waiting for a call. If notified, the hotel operator will transfer your calls to another room, interrupt the call you're on for a more important one, or hold calls while you run out for a soda.

Save money by not paying for things you didn't order. Don't charge anything to your hotel room. It's too confusing to verify the list of room charges when you're checking out. And it's only too easy for the hotel to make a mistake. Most travelers just sign and pay without looking at the list. If you don't charge anything at all, you'll know that extra items on your bill *can't* be yours. *How to do it:* Pay cash for room service, laundry, etc. Use your credit card for food.

And don't depend on the hotel only for information. If you need a service in a strange city (typing, film developing, etc.), call the local convention bureau. It's specifically set up to help out-of-town businesspeople, and there is a convention bureau in every city.

Source: Dr. Barbara A. Pletcher, executive director of the National Association for Professional Saleswomen, Box 255708, Sacramento, CA 95865. She's the author of *Travel Sense,* ACE Books, 51 Madison Ave., New York 10010.

What the Airlines Don't Tell You

•Never accept the first fare quoted. Half the time, some other airline's flight within hours of the one you booked has a special, less expensive deal.

•Take advantage of "illegal" connections. These are connecting flights usually less than 45 minutes apart—too close for airlines to feel safe in making them connect. *Result:* These flights usually do not even show up on the computer when your trip is being routed. *Way out:* Have your agent write up your flight on two separate tickets. The second is for the illegal connection that originates at your transfer point.

Example: You arrive at O'Hare in Chicago on the way to San Francisco. Instead of waiting three hours for the safe connecting flight, you already have a separate ticket from O'Hare to San Francisco on an illegal connection. If you miss the connection, you turn that ticket in for the next available flight. *Cost for two separate tickets:* No more than one through ticket. *Baggage:* Waiting for it to be unloaded can cost you valuable time on this tight schedule. *Best:* Travel with carry-on luggage.

•Some supersaver fares are so low that even if you can't stay as long as their requirements (usually seven days), you will save by buying *two* round-trip tickets—one from your home to your destination for the day you want to leave and one from your destination to your home for the day you want to return. The total may be less than the regular round-trip fare.

•If you miss your flight and there's just time to catch another, go right to the other airline's departure gate instead of to its ticket counter. If it has an empty seat, the second airline will usually honor the ticket for the flight you missed.

•Best seat in the plane. After first class, the choices center on your priorities. For comfort and a smooth ride, pick a seat over the wings. For silence, sit as far forward as possible, but avoid the galley and rest rooms. For legroom, try the first row or seats beside the emergency exits.

•Best way to get a standby seat. Reserve a coach seat for your flight. Arrive at the airport the day you are to leave and see if you can get a standby ticket (Monday, Tuesday, and Wednesday *are the best standby days*). If you do get a standby seat, become a no-show on your reservation (it's built into the price of your ticket) for a full refund. You may win. You can't lose.

Source: *Your Money and Your Life* by Robert Z. Aliber, Basic Books, 10 E. 53 St., New York 10022.

If You Want to Be Bumped To Save the Airfare

Expert bumpees, who have more time than money for traveling, suggest that when you make a reservation on a regularly scheduled airline, you ask if the flight is almost sold out. (Bumping compensation rules don't apply to commuter airlines or charter flights.) Make a reservation only if a flight is almost full. (Pick popular routes at popular times.) Check in 15 minutes prior to boarding, but stay at the end of the line. If the airline asks for volunteers for bumping, speak up. Remember, however, that you don't get a free flight if the airline can get you on another flight for the same destination within the hour.

Source: *You Can Travel Free* by Robert William Kirk, Pelican Publishing Company, 1101 Monroe St., Gretna, LA 70053.

The Most Dangerous Airlines in the World

Based on the number of fatal accidents per million flights, the five airlines with the worst records over a 20-year period (excluding terrorist-related fatalities) are: Aeroflot (USSR)...China Airlines (Taiwan)...Turkish Airlines...EgyptAir...CAAC (China).

Based on the number of fatalities per million passengers, the airlines with the worst records over a 20-year period (excluding terrorist-related deaths) are...Turkish Airlines (124.48 fatalities per million passengers)...Air India (21.48 fatalities)...Avianca (5.93 fatalities)...Nigeria Airways (5.53 fatalities)...LOT Polish Airlines (4.54 fatalities).

Source: *Condé Nast Traveler*, 350 Madison Ave., New York 10017.

The Most Dangerous Airports in the US

Security at major US airports is very poor. Terrorists who are bent on breaching US airport security have ample opportunity to do so in many US cities. *Examples:*

•Los Angeles International Airport. It is possible to walk through several areas marked "Authorized Personnel Only" without being questioned.

•Washington Dulles International Airport. Civilians without ID badges have been able to breach secured zones and walk onto the tarmac close to berthed airplanes.

•San Francisco International Airport. A determined civilian can easily walk through unmarked doors in the terminal, past airline gates, and onto the tarmac among airplanes of numerous different airlines. In one incident, a magazine reporter deliberately failed to show up for a flight to Seoul, South Korea, but airline security didn't notice, and his baggage remained aboard the aircraft.

•New York's JFK International Airport. A civilian can walk onto the tarmac at several locations at this huge airport. In one experiment, an unauthorized person wandered among large aircraft for 10 minutes.

Source: *Condé Nast Traveler*, 360 Madison Ave., New York 10017.

Lost Baggage

The best way to make sure an airline does not lose your baggage: Carry it on the airplane with you. (*Alternative:* Take along less baggage.)

When you must check your bags:

Place name-and-address tags on the inside and outside of each bag. Airlines supply them at ticket counters. (Use a business, not a personal, address.) Remove all old baggage-check tags.

Place a note inside each bag that tells where you are heading on your trip and the dates you will be there.

Lock your bags. It won't prevent theft (luggage keys are often interchangeable), but it will keep a bag from opening accidentally.

Carry on the plane such items as medicine, jewelry, your contact-lens equipment, and any other small, irreplaceable items.

When you check in at the airport, make sure correct baggage checks (for destination and flight number) are attached to your luggage.

Avoid flights during which you change planes and airlines. *Reason:* Transfers account for 40% of lost baggage. If this proves impossible, don't check your baggage through (make arrangements to recheck it between flights).

To minimize the risk of having your baggage stolen, get to the baggage claim area as soon as possible after landing. Put some form of instant identification on your bags to set them apart (a red stripe down the center, or a plaid ribbon).

If your luggage fails to appear, notify the baggage-service personnel immediately. Then fill in the proper tracing form. If you don't file the claim promptly, the airline may deny the loss, particularly if damage is involved.

If your baggage doesn't arrive on the flight you were on, it's likely to show up on the next one. (Ninety-five percent of those that do show up arrive within 24 hours.)

Insurance: The federal government increased the amount per bag for which airlines can be held liable (from $500 to $750). But if your bag and its contents are worth more, consider additional insurance. Buy extra-valuation insurance at the check-in counter. Or get an all-risk policy from your own insurance broker. It covers loss or damage to baggage, along with coverage in the event of illness or accident. Check your homeowner policy for baggage insurance. *Recommended:* Make an inventory describing each bag and its contents. Keep this with you, separate from the baggage.

Traveler Beware

•*Don't fly within 12 hours after dental work.* The change in atmospheric pressure can cause severe pain.

•*First-class air travel.* Not worth the 30% premium unless the flight lasts more than four hours.

•*You shouldn't pay the 8% federal tax on airfare* if you're flying from one US city to another US city in order to catch a flight to another country. You may have to show the agent the foreign ticket.

•*Carry your medical history.* Fold a one-page summary of health data into your passport. *What it should include:* Blood type, allergies, eyeglass prescription, medications currently being taken, any preexisting health condition.

•*Don't buy travel insurance at airports.* Coverage is much more expensive and rates vary from city to city. *Better:* Buy directly from an insurance company.

•*Confirm airline reservations when the small box in the center of the airline ticket is marked "RO."* It indicates that the travel agent has only requested a seat, and wait-listing status is a possibility. A confirmed reservation is indicated by an "OK" on your ticket.

•*Avoid consuming the food and drink offered on airplanes.* Alcohol, nuts, soft drinks, and other foods that have empty calories can cause a swing from high to low blood sugar. You go from feeling great to feeling tired, cramped, and headachy.

•*Alcohol has more punch during an airplane flight than on the ground. Reason:* Body fluids evaporate quickly in the pressurized dry cabin. And under pressure, the alcohol absorbs more fluids in the intestinal tract, thus making itself felt more quickly. *Alternative:* To reduce the dehydration caused by a long flight (six hours or more), drink three or four pints of water during the flight.

Retirement Discount Deals

Reaching 50 or 55 or 60 years of age has its privileges in the marketplace. Businesses want your business, and many are willing to give you a price break to get it if you carry credentials that prove your birth date. Policies do change over time, so always ask about discounts for senior citizens wherever you shop. *Attractive current deals:*

•*Free cruises for single men.* Because unattached males of a certain age are very scarce, two cruise lines offer free travel to single men over 50 who will act as unpaid hosts to the many single women on board the ship. Duties include dancing, serving as dining partners, and mingling with female passengers. No favoritism, no romantic entanglements.

Royal Cruise Lines, Host Program, 1 Maritime Plaza, Suite 1400, San Francisco 94111.
The Delta Queen Steamboat Co., Robin Street Wharf, New Orleans 70130.

•*Great Britain blanket admission.* Great British Heritage Pass is good for admission to more than 600 castles, palaces, homes, and gardens. *Included:* The Tower of London and Windsor Castle.

British Tourist Authority, 40 W. 57 St., New York 10019.

•*Great Britain by rail.* Most European railroads offer senior citizens' discounts. But few can match those in Britain. Passes offer reduced rates on unlimited first-class travel throughout England, Scotland, and Wales. *Note:* Passes must be purchased through a travel agent in the US.

BritRail, 1500 Broadway, Suite 1000, New York 10036.

•*National parks passport.* Golden Age Passport provides free lifetime admission to all of the federal government's parks, monuments, and recreation areas for people over 62. Users also get half off on all fees—camping, boat launching, parking, tours, etc. The pass covers the holder and any passengers in a single-family vehicle.

Not available by mail. Passports can be obtained at any national park where an entrance fee is charged. Proof of age required. More information: National Park Service, Box 37127, Washington, DC 20013.

•*The big discount.* Most airlines, car-rental companies, and hotels offer discounts of 10% or more to travelers over 50. When you make reservations, always ask if a senior citizens' discount is available. *Required:* Some form of identification—a driver's license is usually sufficient.

Warning: Sometimes rates even lower than the senior citizens' discount are offered. Ask if the rate you're getting is the lowest one.

•*Automobile insurance.* State Farm Insurance Company, Nationwide Insurance, Liberty Mutual Insurance Group, Allstate Insurance Company, and AARP (American Association for Retired Persons) all offer special "senior rates" for good drivers.

•*Cruises.* If you are willing to go on short notice, you can get discounts as high as 50%. Check with agencies such as Encore Short Notice (800) 638-8976, Moment's Notice (213) 486-0505, Vacations to Go (800) 624-7338, or Last Minute Travel Club (617) 267-9800.

•*Lodging.* You can stay in homes all over the world for very little or free if you are also willing to take in some senior travelers. INNter Lodging Co-op, Tacoma, WA 98407, (206)756-0343 serves the United States and Canada, and Servas, 11 John St., New York 10038, (212) 267-0252, has an international network of hosts.

•*Retail.* Many stores offer 10% discounts or have special sale days for senior citizens. Check local newspapers for local deals for seniors or simply ask before shopping.

Source: Joan Rattner Heilman, author of *Unbelievably Good Deals & Great Adventures That You Absolutely Can't Get Unless You're Over 50,* Contemporary Books, 180 N. Michigan Ave., Chicago 60601.

Quick Way to Check Hotel Bills

Adjust the amount of the tips so every item that's added to the bill ends with the same digit. *Example:* Tip odd amounts to have the bills for all meals end with the numeral six. It takes only a moment to skim the list for items that don't end in six, and thus don't belong on your bill. The odds of an accidental six occurring on the bill are nine-to-one in favor of the traveler.

Second Passports: The State Department's Best-Kept Secret

Some countries won't permit entry to travelers whose passports show that they've previously visited certain other countries. Most Arab countries, for example, won't allow entry to people whose passports have a stamp showing that they've visited Israel. A similar situation confronts people traveling among some African countries. Traveling freely among these countries is a matter of carrying two passports and knowing when to use them.

You can get a *second* passport, a *restricted passport.* It looks just like a regular US passport, with one exception...it clearly states that it is limited to use for travel to specific countries. The restricted passport can't be substituted for a regular passport. It can't be used to enter every country, only the ones that are specified on the application. And it isn't issued for countries with which the United States has no diplomatic relations.

Apply for one at your regional passport office, but be prepared to document your legitimate need...itinerary, assignment from your employer specifying that you need to do business in a particular country, etc. Take two signed passport-sized photos.

To find out if you'll need a restricted passport, check the Visa Information Sheet available from any passport office. That document will help you to determine if there are visa or passport conflicts among the countries on your itinerary. *Extra protection:* Check with the consulate or embassy of each country you plan to visit.

Reason: Customs regulations of foreign governments change so quickly that even the State Department is unable to keep its information on these regulations absolutely up-to-date.

Avoid relying on information from travel agencies. They use the "Travel Information Manual" put out by an airline organization. Because the compiling, distribution, etc., can take a long time, the manual can be out-of-date as soon as it's issued.

While traveling, be sure to stay on top of possible entry-rule changes at borders you plan to cross. If entrance to a country depends on the restricted passport, show only *that* document. Put away your regular passport. Using two passports is officially frowned upon by most governments, so there could be repercussions.

If you use the wrong passport on arrival, you'll probably be refused entry. If you're caught with the wrong document when leaving, on the other hand, chances are the border guards will let you depart.

Very, very important: The restricted passport may not be honored by some countries. If it isn't, contact the nearest US embassy or consulate for emergency assistance.

Source: Privileged information from our insiders at the US State Department.

Preventing Montezuma's Revenge

University of Texas Medical School researchers have discovered that the primary ingredient in Pepto-Bismol (bismuth subsalicylate) can help to prevent the most common traveler's ailment. A group of new students in Mexico received four tablespoons of the medication four times a day (for 21 days). Others were given a placebo. Diarrhea developed in only 14 of 62 students on medication versus 40 of 66 students on the placebo.

Getting the Best for Less at Hotels

Experienced travelers who are flexible can usually get a deal on hotel rooms by waiting until the last minute to make their reservations. This doesn't work when a major event has every hotel room in a city booked weeks in advance, but during slow economic times or seasonal slumps, it's worth a try. *What you do:* The day you want the room, call the specific hotel you want (not the chain 800 number). Ask for the assistant manager and explain that you want to stay at the hotel but would like to know what kind of a deal can be made. If a suite is the only thing available, you'll get it for room rates or you may get discounts of up to 50%, which is much better for the hotel than an empty, nonpaying room.

Source: *Money*, Rockefeller Center, New York 10020.

Outwitting Hotel Thieves

•Don't use a "pickproof" lock in hotel-room drawers. This tells the burglar precisely where your valuables are.

Good place to hide things in a hotel room: Under the rug, under the bed. If it's difficult for you to get to, it will also be difficult for a burglar.

•Don't drop off your room key at the desk while you're away—until you check out.

•Request duplicate room key.

•When you go out, leave a light and the TV on in the room.

•Whenever you leave your car, lock it and take your valuables with you. If you're parking in a garage that has an attendant, don't leave the key for the trunk.

•Don't put all your cash or traveler's checks in one place or one pocket. Having traveler's checks replaced involves inconvenience.

Duty-Free Shops

Check the prices at duty-free shops against prices in local stores. Airport and dockside shops generally charge higher, rather than prevailing, prices for their products. In addition, top-of-the-line products are sold, meaning that the prices are high to begin with.

So buy only otherwise heavily taxed items in these stores. Liquor, cigarettes, perfume, and some wines may still be bargains.

Source: *Travel Smart*, 40 Beechdale Rd., Dobbs Ferry, NY 10522.

Choosing a Vacation Cruise

Focus on a cruise with a compatible group. People over 60 generally take longer cruises. People on summer cruises are usually 15 to 20 years *younger* than those on winter cruises.

Compare the capacity of the ship's main lounge with the number of passengers. If the lounge is relatively small, there will be uncomfortable fast meals and guests will scramble for seats at entertainment performances.

Seasick avoidance: Get a cabin as close to the center of the ship as possible, on the middle deck, off the main corridor.

Luxury-Cruise Bargains

Luxury cruises at 50% to 60% off are often available if you can be flexible about when you go. Find several cruises that look good to you, then wait until the last minute. Get your travel agent to call and see if there are any last-minute vacancies; if there are, you can usually have them for just over cost.

Source: Robert William Kirk, *You Can Travel Free*, Pelican Publishing Company, 1101 Monroe St., Gretna, LA 70053.

Cruise Ship Rapes: Uncensored Facts

Three out of every four crimes on cruise ships reported to the US Attorney's Office in Miami are sexual offenses.

Most involve young women—under 21.

But crimes at sea are hard to prosecute. They may go unreported, the evidence may be old, and potential witnesses scatter as soon as the ship docks. Most complaints from passengers involve crew members. A cruise company official admits that although they do try to make background checks, it is very difficult.

Bottom line: Although the great majority of cruises are well managed and safe, passengers need to be cautious. Women in particular should not walk the decks and inner corridors of a cruise ship alone, nor should parents allow their children to roam unescorted.

Source: US Attorney's Office in Miami.

Pros and Cons of Group Travel Tours

Best reason to choose a package tour: Economy. Savings can amount to several hundred dollars per couple. The food and drink on chartered jets tends to be better than on commercial flights, but space is more cramped. Chartered air-conditioned buses between airports and train stations are a big convenience and eliminate the need for constant tipping in foreign currency. *Warning: Chartered deluxe European express trains* are pleasant but by no means *express*. They are frequently sidetracked for the *real* express trains.

Tours also save time on planning and organizing and are especially helpful to those who have not traveled to a country before or do not speak the language.

Minuses for package tours: Rushed sightseeing schedule. Be wary of promises of *full American breakfasts*. They're usually of poor quality. It's probably better to stick with a traditional roll and coffee in Europe.

Tip: Save coupon books for gourmet dinners at restaurants on special nights. Pay cash for light suppers when you're tired or have had a late lunch.

Best tour to pick: One sponsored by a local professional, cultural, or educational group. It usually assures you of finding compatible companions.

Tipping Guide

Restaurant tipping guidelines from restaurateurs Vincent Sardi (of Sardi's) and Tom Margittai (co-owner of the Four Seasons):

• *Waiter:* Fifteen percent of the bill (not including tax).

• *Captain:* Five percent. *Note:* If diner writes tip on the check, the *waiter gets it all*, unless the diner specifies how it is to be split. (*Example:* Waiter, $5; captain, $2.)

• *Headwaiter who seats diners:* Five dollars or $10 or more at intervals for regular patrons. He should be tipped in cash.

• *Sommelier:* Ten percent of the wine selection or 5% if the wine is expensive. Two dollars or $3 is a good tip.

• *Bartender:* One dollar minimum or 15% of check.

• *Hatcheck:* Fifty cents to $1 per couple.

• *Rest-room attendant:* Fifty cents.

• *Doorman* (to get taxi): Fifty cents normally. One dollar in bad weather or rush hour.

• *Other staff at a restaurant that is used regularly should be tipped once or twice a year:* Hosts, switchboard operators (where the restaurant provides telephone service).

• *Nightclubs:* Headwaiter should get $2 to $10 per person, depending on the impression the party host wishes to make on his guests. (Higher tip usually ensures better service.)

Other tipping:

• *Limousine service:* Fifteen percent to the driver. If service charge is included in bill, tip an additional $5.

• *Hotels:* Valet, room service, bartender, should get about 50 cents, depending on the amount and quality of service. Bellman: Fifty cents per bag. Chambermaid: One dollar per day.

•*Sports arenas and racetracks:* A $5 tip to an usher will often give you and your guests access to unused reserved seats.

Best Gambling

Craps and baccarat offer the best shot that Las Vegas casinos give. They take the smallest percentage and are easiest to play. Blackjack is the game for those with a sharp eye and a good memory. *Worst bets:* Keno, roulette, and slot machines (in that order). Atlantic City roulette odds are better than Nevada houses but not as good as French casinos. The best blackjack is in Las Vegas, the worst in Atlantic City. The best craps rules are in Great Britain.

Insider's Guide to Casino Gambling

As a weekend gambler, you're basically out for a good time. The odds are you won't break the bank. But you *can* enhance your enjoyment—and maybe even take home some house money—if you follow a few general rules.

•*Go in with a game plan and stick to it.* Decide in advance how much money you're going to take, how much you can afford to lose, and at what point you will quit.

•*Limit each bet to 1% of your original stake.* That may be as little as $5 (the weekend minimum in Atlantic City). Up your bets *only* when you are ahead. Never bet more than 10% of the stake. If you start chasing money you've lost, the odds of going broke are much higher. That's the wrong approach to gambling.

•*Don't push your luck.* If you've won $100 with a given dealer and then lose $20 of your profits, back off. Take a deep breath or break for dinner. In any case, find a new table.

•*Pass up the free drinks.* Casinos offer them for a reason. If you lose your inhibitions, you may desert your strategy and change your betting patterns. You want to keep a clear head.

Blackjack

This is the best casino game—the only one in which a skilled player can beat the house over time. Overall, of course, the casinos make a nice profit because their edge against the average "hunch" player runs from 6% to 15%.

However, with an advanced card-counting system, the odds are turned around. The experienced player has a 2% advantage. Mastery of the counting system takes time and practice. A simplified version gives the player a 15% edge, but it still requires instruction and some dedicated use.

For the recreational gambler, a basic blackjack strategy—with *no* counting—can cut the house edge to only .4%. Given those odds, you'd lose about $2 in an average hour if you bet $4 per hand—not a bad entertainment value.

Rules for the no-count system:

•Never split pairs of 4s, 5s, or 10s. Always split aces and 8s. Split other pairs if the dealer's up card is 2 through 6.

•Double your bet on 11 unless the dealer shows an ace. Double on 10 unless the dealer shows an ace or a 10. Double on 9 if the dealer shows 3 through 6 and on soft hands (hands with an ace that can be counted as 11 without going over 21) of 13 through 18 if the dealer shows 4 through 6.

•Always stand on hard hands (hands with no ace or an ace that must be counted as 1) of 17 and up. Stand on hands of 12 through 16 if the dealer shows 2 through 6. (Otherwise, hit.) Always stand on soft hands of 18 and up. Always hit on soft hands of 17 or less if it is too late to double.

These rules will keep you out of serious trouble. But human nature being what it is, you will naturally want to play an occasional hunch against the odds. *Best hunch to bet:* An "insurance" bet on the dealer's hand when you have been dealt a blackjack. *Reason:* When you have a blackjack, the only thing that can keep you from winning is the dealer also having a blackjack. An insurance bet on his cards assures you of getting *something* on the hand.

Craps

This is the most emotional casino game. Fast and noisy, it can sweep you into making more bets per hour than other games—as many as 150. *Result:* The money turns over faster and you lose more. However, if you stick to the most favorable bets, you concede an edge of only .8% to the house.

Bets to make: Pass line. Don't pass. Come. Don't come. In each case, always make the maximum accompanying "odds" bets (these offer the best percentage of all). The only other acceptable wagers are "place" bets on 6 or 8 (the house edge on these is 1.4%).

Avoid all long-shot and one-roll bets like "hardway 4." The stick man will encourage this action because it makes money for the casino. The odds against you are enormous, because the house advantage runs from 10% to 16%.

Under the rules of probability, there is *no* true number system to help the craps gambler. Each roll of the dice is independent. But there are useful betting strategies. *A good one:* After the roller has thrown two passes (winning rolls), up your bet 50% every *other* pass thereafter.

Roulette

Number systems will do you no good in roulette. The general house edge is high: 5.3%. To halve your disadvantage, stick to "outside" even-money bets: Red-black. Odd-even. High-low. If 0 or 00 comes up, you lose only half of these wagers. Other bets are lost in full.

Baccarat

Although the house edge is only 1.1%, this "upper crust" game gives the player no control. *You make only two decisions:* How much you want to put down and your preference for the banker or the player.

Baccarat players tend to be superstitious, and they are notorious for being streak players.

Warning: The baccarat minimum is generally pretty high—$20 to $25. This makes it an expensive game to play.

Final Shot

Let's say you've doubled your initial stake and you have time for one more session before the weekend is over. *Don't be greedy.* Just as you set a strict loss limit (say, 20% of your stake) and stop at it, you should quit while you are ahead, too. Enjoy the sights and the shows, and go home with your profit. If everyone did that, the casinos would be in trouble.

Gambling Trap

Never accept a check to cover a gambling debt. If the check bounces, the amount is not collectible in a court of law. This is true even in states where gambling is legal.

Source: Jerry L. Patterson, director of Jerry Patterson's Blackjack Clinic, 1 Britton Place, Voorhees, NJ 08043, and the author of *Casino Gambling*, Perigee Books, 200 Madison Ave., New York 10016.

Test for Loaded Dice

Fill a tall glass with water and drop each die in gently. Repeat several times, with a different number on top each time. If each die turns when sinking so that the same two or three numbers always show up, it's loaded. *Less obvious test:* Hold the die loosely between the thumb and forefinger at diagonally opposite corners. Loaded dice will pivot when the weighted side is on top. The movement is unmistakable.

How to Spot a Card Cheat

If you suspect marked cards, riffle the deck and watch the design on the back. If the cards are marked, some lines in the design will move like an animated cartoon. In an honest deck, the design will stand absolutely still. *The player to suspect:* The one who keeps his eyes glued to the back of the cards—especially the hole card in the game stud poker and the top card of the deck in the game gin rummy.

Source: *John Scarne's Newsletter.*

How to Turn Slot-Machine Odds in Your Favor

The odds of winning on slot machines almost invariably favor the casino. But—with the proper strategies—you can increase your chances of striking it rich with one lucky pull.

Key factor: The machine's payback percentage...the proportion of the money wagered that is returned to the players over the long run. If the payback is 95%, the machine returns $95 for every $100 wagered—with $5 held as casino profit.

If the payback is 85%, the machine would return only $85, with $15 going to the casino. A higher payback percentage will help conserve your stake and make it less likely that you'll "bust" before your casino visit or vacation is over. At the same time, it will allow you more opportunities to hit a big jackpot.

- Best place to play: Las Vegas, where the payback runs 92%–97%.
- Next best: Reno, at 92%–95%.
- Least favorable: Atlantic City, at 85%–92%.

In Las Vegas, the best machines of all can be found at large casinos off the Strip (Las Vegas Boulevard), such as Sam's Town, the Gold Coast, the Santa Fe, and the Showboat. These casinos cater less to tourists and more to discerning local players, who will go wherever the odds are most favorable.

100+% payback: In their never-ending game of one-upmanship, several off-the-Strip casinos are now offering slot machines that pay back more than 100%. The longer you play at this type of machine, the more you can expect to win.

The catch: There is no way of telling where these machines are located.

On the other hand, if you find a near-deserted bank of machines in an otherwise busy casino, there's probably a good reason...the players have migrated to where the paybacks are better.

Advice: If you have a choice, play where there are a lot of people and where it's busy.

Wherever they gamble, too many slot players are led astray by popular myths.

•Myth No. 1: Play the machine nearest the door or on the aisle. Years ago, casinos might have tried to attract passing tourists by placing their higher payback-percentage machines in high-traffic areas. But the machines have now become so popular that casinos have no need for such tactics.

Fact: The only reason to play a machine on an aisle is for comfort, as you won't be crowded by other players on either side of you.

•Myth No. 2: If the machine pays back with hot coins, it's a "hot" machine.

Fact: Coins come out of some machines hotter than others because of their proximity to lights or other electrical components in the machine. Their temperature has nothing to do with the machine's payback percentage.

•Myth No. 3: "I've put so much money in it, it has to be ready to hit." Today's slot machines are controlled by microprocessors. These miniature computers generate random outcomes of winning or losing symbols according to the millisecond that you insert your coin or pull your handle. There is no such thing as a "pay cycle" or "cold cycle" on these machines. Each play is independent of the next. Since jackpots are produced by timing, rather than any given number of pulls, there is no way to predict when a machine is more likely to "hit."

Let's say you play a machine for an hour and lose $50 before you end your session. As you collect what's left of your stake, another player pulls the handle of "your" machine and hits a four-figure jackpot on his very first try. Before you start cursing your luck, remember—had you stayed to play, the odds are overwhelming that you wouldn't have won that jackpot. The hit was triggered not by the pull of the handle but by the precise timing of the play.

•Myth No. 4: If a machine isn't paying, stop playing the maximum number of coins. Drop down to one coin and increase your bet to the maximum when the machine "warms up" again.

Fact: You should always play the maximum number of coins (generally between two and five), for the simple reason that the top jackpots award a significant bonus for maximum plays. If you play less than the maximum, you'll be donating an extra 2%–5% advantage to the house.

Strategy: If you can't afford to play the maximum, drop down to a lower-denomination machine.

Example: It's more advantageous to play four quarters (assuming that's the maximum) than one quarter on a machine with a $1 maximum.

Smart Money Strategies

The most successful slots players are those who are disciplined in their money management:

•Set a strict gambling "budget" for your trip—a sum you can afford to lose without guilt or hardship.

•Divide your stake by the number of days you plan to play. If you've budgeted $300 for a three-day weekend, you can risk no more than $100 per day.

•Set a time limit for each session (an hour or two is reasonable) and buy a limited number of coins—say, $25 in quarters.

•Don't play back any coins that drop in the tray. Use only your original "buy." When those coins run out, take stock of what's in your tray. If you're ahead, cash in at the change booth and place your profit in the "winning section" of your purse or wallet. This money is untouchable. If you're behind, add whatever you have left to your original stake.

•If you're behind, take a break. If you're ahead, buy more change with another portion of your original stake and play that out. Proceed as above.

•If you've played half your stake and lost most or all of it, change your game plan. Change to a lesser-denomination machine (quarters instead of dollars, nickels instead of quarters, three-coin instead of five-coin).

•If you're ahead and your machine keeps you ahead with each cash-in, keep playing. But once your last cash-in amount is considerably less than the amount of stake spent, it's time to move on to a new machine—if only for psychological reasons.

•If you've played your allotted time and still have some of your original session stake, consider yourself lucky. Move what's left to your "winnings" pocket. This money is also untouchable—never bet your winnings!

Bottom Line

If you play on indefinitely for a big jackpot without conserving your smaller wins, the casino's advantage is almost sure to wipe you out.

Even if you eventually hit your jackpot, it's unlikely to outweigh your accumulated losses. You must accept every win, no matter how large, for what it is—a victory against the odds.

Source: Dwight Crevelt, a senior engineer on the technical staff at IGT, a Las Vegas slot machine manufacturer. He is the co-author (with his mother, Louise Crevelt) of *Slot Machine Mania* and has a second book, *Video Poker Mania*. Both are published by Gollehon Press

Best Casino Deals

All casinos aren't alike in the odds they offer,

and there can even be important differences among neighboring tables in the same house. Nevada casinos vary widely from one another...more than do houses in Atlantic City.

Example: In Vegas, craps tables might list the odds on a "2 or 12" roll as 30 to 1—on a $1 bet, the croupier will return $31 to you. Or the odds might be listed as 30 to 1—a winning bet of $1 returns only $30. The odds are clearly marked on the table, but the casinos count on you not to read the fine print so they can earn what amounts to a free dollar on the 30 to 1 odds.

In Vegas, the best deals are usually found in the smaller casinos in the Fremont Street–downtown area, away from the fabled Strip. *Big caution:* The more out-of-the-way the casino, the greater your chances of being cheated by crooked dealers. Be especially wary of blackjack games, because in Nevada all cards are dealt by hand.

Source: Lee Pantano, syndicated gambling columnist, consultant, and director of the nation's only school for advanced baccarat card counting. He's also the publisher of the casino newsletter *Gamblegram.*

Security

Protecting Yourself Against Muggers

The best defense against becoming a crime victim is to avoid a setup. Muggers, like most people, don't take more risks or work harder than they have to. *Point:* They choose victims who seem easy to handle. And they create situations that make the attack simpler.

Chief defense: Don't allow yourself to be distracted, isolated, or simply stopped on the street by a stranger. Muggers prefer victims who have stopped moving. They use every technique to accomplish that: asking for directions, a match, or a handout.

First and most important rule: If you're spoken to by a suspicious stranger, don't stop. Move away quickly. Don't slow down to watch an argument or any other commotion on the street. Fake street fights are a favorite way to set up a robbery.

Defensive tactics: Walk down the sidewalk near the street. Be wary of corners and doorways. Reduce the possibility of being grabbed from the shadows. Hugging the curb permits you to see around the corner while at a distance. Be alert to someone hiding between or behind parked cars.

Walk a couple of extra blocks to take a safe route, especially late at night. Keep to known neighborhoods. Identify in advance where the places of refuge are, in event of trouble.

Look ahead up the street (not down) to see what's happening. Be alert, especially to people loitering or moving suspiciously. *Example:* Two men up ahead who suddenly separate and begin walking apart. They could be preparing to set you up.

However foolish or rude it may seem, don't get on a self-service elevator if there's somebody on it who looks at all suspicious. Never let an elevator you are on go to the basement. *How to avoid it:* When entering an open elevator, keep a foot in the door while pressing the floor number. Keep your eyes on the elevator indicator. If the arrow points down, don't get in.

Don't get into a self-service elevator late at night without making sure that nobody is waiting on an upper floor to intercept you. *How to do it:* Push the top elevator button, but don't get in. If the elevator does not stop on any floor on the way up or down, it's safe.

Avoid places where gangs of juveniles congregate. They can be more dangerous than professional muggers because they will often hurt a victim rather than take the money and run.

Get into the habit of automatically saying excuse me when you bump into someone on the street. Say it no matter whose fault it is.

Never show money in public, whether at a newsstand, market, bank, or getting out of a cab. Muggers are watching.

If you are mugged:

Cooperate. Above all, communicate the willingness to cooperate. Keep calm. It can help relax the mugger, too, which is crucial. *Reason:* If a mugger is pointing a cocked revolver, nervousness on his/her part could be fatal to you. *Ways to calm the situation:* Say something reassuring, or ask a distracting question that establishes the mugging as a businesslike transaction. *Example:* You can have anything you want. Do you mind if I just keep my driver's license?

Never move suddenly. Tell the mugger where your wallet is and ask: Do you want me to get it, or do you want to get it?

A woman mugger with a knife or gun can kill just as easily as a man. Letting macho feelings interfere with cooperating can be suicidal.

Don't show the slightest condescension or hostility. Be careful of your tone of voice. Cooperating with disdain can set off violence. *Best attitude to project:* You've got to earn a living, too. Or: I don't hold this against you at all; times are tough.

Don't make jokes. They are too risky, and the chance for misinterpretation is too great.

Avoid direct or steady eye contact.

If a mugger is particularly hostile, be super-cooperative. Offer money or possessions he has overlooked.

Bottom line: Always carry mugger money. Keep $25 to $100 in your pocket as insurance. A happy mugger is much less likely to do harm than one who comes away empty-handed.

If you are attacked in the hallway of a hotel or an apartment building, yelling for help often won't bring assistance. People who hear you may be too afraid to come out of their doors, worrying that the attacker is armed. Smarter: Yell, "Fire!" Most people will rush into the hall for their own safety, and your attacker will be frightened off by sheer numbers.

Source: Ken Glickman, director, Seido Self-Defense, 61 W. 23 St., New York 10010.

What a Burglar Thinks About Burglar-Alarm Systems

Michael Weaver, in Walla Walla prison, tells what he learned about burglar alarms in his years of dealing with them professionally—*mostly* successfully. *His from-behind-bars report:*

Systems to Avoid

•*Door and window alarms.* They are usually turned on by key when the last person leaves the premises. The alarm systems monitor all the doors and windows. If anyone tries to open them, an alarm sounds. *These systems aren't only worthless, they are an invitation to the burglar. Reason:* They are visible (tape on windows and contact points around doors), so the burglar knows what he has to deal with. He may simply enter and leave through a roof vent, or he may use a jumper wire to "fool" the electrical system.

•*Electronic eye alarms:* These rate no better than door and window alarms. They operate like automatic supermarket doors. When an invisible beam is broken, a silent alarm is tripped. Since the eye can be moved and aimed easily, it can be shifted to cover doors, windows, walls, or a safe. Like door and window alarms, these systems are easy to breach using optical equipment to discover their position from a safe vantage point. Once the burglar spots them, he just works around them.

Effective Alarms

•*Proximity alarms:* Usually, they are activated by noise. Microphones are placed throughout an area and activated when the premises are empty. They are sensitive to any noise they are programmed to register. They are generally very effective. *One weakness:* The last person to leave will activate the system. If anyone wishes to return, he/she must telephone the monitor, giving a code number and the length of time he expects to be in. If a burglar spots this kind of activity, he may (among other things) place a miniature recorder near the phone and learn the code. *Solution:* Code numbers, security information, and schedules must be protected and changed frequently.

Tip: If you're shopping for an alarm, check out systems used by drugstores in your area. They are generally the best.

Key and Safe Advice

As vulnerable as they are, keys are the most cost-effective security device. *Ways to make those keys significantly more secure:*

•Stamp "Do Not Duplicate" on keys. It's not foolproof, but it helps to hinder unauthorized key copying.

•Use locks that require very hard-to-get key blanks. Some blanks are secure; that is, licensed keymakers don't stock the blanks; they must be acquired from the lock maker. There is a delay—not long, but worthwhile.

•Many lock combinations (those that can be adjusted) are set to the user's birthday, Social Security number, phone number, or some other obvious set of digits. And crooks know that. In "casing" a potential burglary site, sophisticated thieves gather all the obvious numbers and usually open the safe quite easily.

If none of the numbers work, the burglar looks in the "obvious" places for hiding the number: In the executive's diary or calendar, under the desk pad.

Recommendation: Don't use a related number. Memorize the digits, and don't put them in "safe" places.

•*Signatures.* For important papers, sign your name in ink and with an *italic* pen. It's very hard to forge.

How to Spot a Fake ID

Best identification: Photograph, physical description, and signature. *Other safeguards:*

Repeat some information from the ID card back to the holder, but make a small mistake in repetition. *Example:* Is your address 733 Lake Dr.? (743 is the real number.) Impostors are often unfamiliar with details.

Don't accept IDs that have the name of the state or issuing agency typed in instead of printed. Also, a typographical error is almost always a sign of a fake.

Check wear patterns on old cards. A genuine card will be worn mostly around the edges from handling. Some forgers artificially age cards, which gives them a uniform look of wear.

Look for raised edges around photographs, which is a sign that a substitution has been made.

Feel for flaws in laminated cards, another sign of tampering.

Compare the typewriter face on various parts of the card. Reject it if there is a mismatch.

Check the holder's signature against the one on the ID.

Beware: Birth certificates are poor IDs because they fail to describe the adult using them. *Better:* A driver's license, passport, or credit card (that can be checked to see if stolen).

Source: *The National Notary Magazine.*

Before You Buy a Safe

Most home safes on the market today are designed to protect against either fire or theft, but not both. So, the best solution is to buy one of each type. Manufacturers suggest welding the theft safe inside the fire safe, then bolting the whole thing to a concrete wall or floor.

What to look for:

Burglar-resistant safes. You generally get what you pay for. Minimum advisable specifications: A half-inch-thick solid steel door and quarter-inch-thick solid steel walls. (*Aim:* To prevent a thief from peeling away the walls with a crowbar.) *Also:* Make sure the safe has a relocking device in addition to a good-quality lock. If the lock is tampered with, the device automatically relocks the bolts.

Fire-resistant safes. Recommended for most homes: A safe that can withstand a temperature of 1,850°F for two hours.

Prices depend on the size of the safe, the specifications of the materials, or the rating of the model. And for burglar-resistant safes, the complexity of locks and relocking devices adds to the cost.

Money saver: A used safe. The cost is 20% to 40% lower than comparable new safes.

Eleven Professional Techniques Used by Private Investigators

In every state it is legal for you to be your own private investigator. No license or permission from anyone or any government agency is required. You must not, however, *represent* yourself as a private investigator.

Much of the information you will ever want or need to know about any person or property can easily be obtained in your city or county hall of records or county courthouse when you know where and how to look.

Information recorded in halls of records and county courthouses is public information.

Here is a list of 11 easy ways to obtain information:

•The Registrar of Voters, also known as the Board of Elections, is one of the very best sources of information. A person's date of birth, height, color of eyes, place of employment, previous address, immigration information, and even nonpublished telephone number is available through the Registrar of Voters.

•The Department of Motor Vehicles is another source of information. You can obtain the identification of all vehicles owned by an individual as well as the person's driving record, including all license suspensions, and a copy of all ownership records.

•Under the Freedom of Information Act, the name of any particular box holder, current address, and a forwarding address, if he/she has moved within one year, is available from any post office. The fee is $1. However, for the same fee, an individual can request that this information not be provided to others.

•Property records. There is one property records office per county. Records include many types of information relating to real estate. For example, records of deeds, judgments, and tax liens.

•Tax assessor/tax collector. This is a good place to look for records concerning anyone who may be responsible for payment of taxes on real or personal property.

•Bureau of vital statistics. This office catalogs birth, death, and marriage records.

•Reverse phone directories. Many phone companies sell reverse directories listing subscribers by telephone number and address. If you have the number, you can get the name and address of the subscriber. You can also get a phone number, and a name, by looking up the address. Unlisted numbers do not appear in this book.

•Medical associations. These organizations will confirm an individual's license to practice and the specialties in which he/she has been board certified.

•Colleges and universities. Alumni offices will usually confirm the graduation or attendance of particular individuals, including the year the person graduated and degrees, if any.

•Credit bureaus. Dun and Bradstreet, TRW, or local credit bureaus will not provide information unless the inquirer is a subscriber and can give the appropriate code number and is prepared to pay a fee.

•Local court records.

Source: *How to Be Your Own Private Detective* by Vincent Parco, Tresco Inc., Canton, OH 44703.

Retirement Planning

Arithmetic to Do Before You Retire

How to size up your financial situation:

1. List your assets. Include income-producing assets (stocks, bonds, other annuity-generating insurance policies, real estate, company profit-sharing plans), plus nonincome-producing assets (paid-up life insurance, furniture, and household goods) and assets that require expenditures for maintenance (houses, cars, etc.). Estimate total dollar value, factoring in appreciation.

2. Figure out postretirement income. Add up income from assets, pensions, and Social Security.

3. Calculate postretirement expenses, then deduct costs stemming from work (commuting, clothes). Next, add on the cost of benefits (health insurance) that will no longer be covered by an employer. Estimate an annual dollar figure. Factor in the inflation rate.

4. If postretirement expenses outstrip postretirement income, develop a plan for liquidating assets. *Rule of thumb:* The percentage of total capital that a retired person may spend annually begins at 5% at age 65 and increases by 1% every five years until he/she reaches 8% at age 80.

Bottom line: Only those whose postretirement expenses still outstrip total income at this point will have to cut back. Generally, a retired person needs 75% of his preretirement, after-tax income to maintain his present standard of living.

Pension Bigger Than Salary

A provision in ERISA (the 1974 pension law) makes it possible for a small, closely held corporation to provide its older insiders, in a relatively short time, with pension benefits substantially larger than their compensation—and with the cost fully deductible by the corporation.

Example: A Mr. Smith, having elected early retirement from a major corporation, starts his own consulting corporation. He brings his wife into the business as an assistant and has two part-time employees to help her with various chores. He puts his wife on the books for $6,000 a year, although she's worth more. Even though he considers increasing her pay, he has prudent misgivings, because her earnings will only add to the taxable income on their joint return.

Taking advantage of ERISA, Smith sets up a defined-benefit pension plan (where benefit payout is fixed) for his corporation. Under the so-called *de minimis* provisions of ERISA, he can set his wife's defined benefit upon retirement at $10,000 a year—$4,000 more than her annual salary. She's able to escape the benefit limit of 100% of her annual salary because her salary is under $10,000.

To establish the $10,000 benefit, Smith must show actuarially what it would cost to provide his wife with a straight-life annuity of $10,000 a year at age 65. That's easy. All he has to do is ask a life insurance company how much such a policy would cost. *Answer:* $140,000 lump sum. Thus, if you figure an 8% annual interest, compounded, it works out that he must put away $10,000 a year for the next 10 years—or a total of $100,000. Additionally, Mrs. Smith has to participate in the plan for 10 years. Otherwise the $10,000 will be reduced.

What was done was to provide Mrs. Smith with a benefit worth $140,000 with $100,000 in tax-deductible dollars.

Another plus: If those dollars had been paid to Mrs. Smith as straight compensation (and assuming that Mr. and Mrs. Smith filed joint returns), she would have paid out a large sum in taxes over the next 10 years of employment by the corporation.

How Safe Is Your Pension?

How to check on the safety of your retirement income:

For employees of public companies: Basic information is included in the firm's annual report. Usually the size of a firm's unfunded pension liability and the size of its past service liability are disclosed in footnotes. More detailed information is available in the financial section of the firm's 10K report, filed with the Securities and Exchange Commission.

For employees of private companies: Anyone who is in a qualified plan (one approved by the IRS under the code) has the right to obtain information about his/her pension from the trustees of the plan. They may be either internal or external trustees. The average person may not be able to decipher the information. If you can't, take it to a pension expert, actuary, lawyer, or accountant for an analysis. *Cost:* $500–$800. Whether you are examining the pension information of public or private firms, you are seeking the same kind of basic information.

Principle: The size of a company's liability for retirement payouts is not as important as the assumptions about funding these liabilities. Like a mortgage, these obligations don't exist 100% in the present. Concern yourself with *how* the company expects to fund its liabilities.

Types of Liabilities

•*Unfunded pension liabilities.* The amount a firm expects to need over the next 20–30 years to supply vested workers with promised pension benefits. These figures are derived from various actuarial assumptions.

•*Past service liabilities.* Created when a company raises its pension compensation. For instance, a company may have been planning to provide 40% of compensation as a pension. One year, it may raise that to 45% and treat it retroactively.

Trouble Signs

•*A poor record on investing.* Compare the market value of the assets in the pension with their book value. If book value is more than market value, the trustees have not been investing wisely. *Point:* If the fund had to sell those assets today, there would be a loss. You might also get a bit nervous if the fund is still holding some obscure bonds or other fixed-income obligations issued at low rates years ago.

•*Funding assumptions are overstated.* Actuaries have a myriad of estimates on how long it takes to fund pension plans and what rate of return a company will get. *What to look at:*

Time frame: This should not be long. If the firm is funding over 40 years, you will want to know why and how, since 10–20 years is more customary. *Reason:* We don't have a crystal ball, and the investment world will be different in as little as 10 years from now. Assumptions made on 40 years may not hold up at all.

Rate of return: If a company assumes a conservative 6%–7% or less right now, you can be comfortable. If the assumed rate is 10% or more, you will want to know how it plans to meet that expectation for the entire fund over the long run.

Salary and wage scales: The company should be assuming an increase in compensation over years. Most plans have such provisions. They must start funding now for future salary increases.

Assumptions about the employee turnover rate: These should be consistent with the historically documented turnover of the company. If a firm has a very low turnover rate and assumes a 4% turnover, the company will be underfunded at some time. Estimates should be conservative.

To assess your own status in a corporate pension plan, see *how many years you have been vested.*

Many people have the illusion that they are fully vested for maximum pensions after only five years or so. In truth, companies couldn't afford to fully vest people with such short service. They may offer some token pension for such service. But most people are not fully vested until they have worked for the firm for 10 or even 20 years, and then they might be vested only to the extent of their accrued pension to date, not the full pension expected at normal retirement. With so much job-hopping in the past two decades, an individual's pension-fund status may be much less than is imagined.

Employees of troubled or even bankrupt companies need not panic. The trustees of the plan have an obligation to the vested employees. The assets of the plan are segregated, and no creditor can reach them. In fact, as a creditor, the corporate pension plan can grab some corporate assets under certain circumstances. And if there has been gross mismanagement of pension funds, the stockholders of a closely held company can be held personally liable.

Source: James E. Conway, president of the Ayco Corporation, a consulting firm specializing in executive finances, 1 Wall St., Albany, NY 12205.

An IRA Loophole That Sounds Almost Too Good to Be Legal

Contributions to an IRA must be in *cash only* (since 1987, gold or silver coins of the US can be used), not stocks, bonds, or other property. And if you sell anything to raise your contribution, you must pay tax on any capital gain. *Tip:* Sell stocks that have *declined* in value. You can fund the IRA and also get a capital loss on the sale. Furthermore, if you desire, your IRA can repurchase the stocks immediately. The wash- sale rules shouldn't apply, as you and your IRA are separate legal entities.

Borrow from Your Own Retirement Plan and Pay Yourself Deductible Interest

Pay interest to yourself, deduct part of the interest you pay, then *receive the same interest tax-free*. Sounds weird—but this tax-saving strategy makes sense—dollars and cents.

How: Borrow from your own qualified retirement plan. The IRS says that this is possible even when the plan covers only a *single* company employee. However, key employees aren't allowed to deduct the interest on these loans.

Requirements:

•The plan must specifically allow borrowing to all covered employees on a nondiscriminatory basis.

•The loan must bear a reasonable rate of interest, be adequately secured, and be repaid within five years. *Exception to the five-year rule:* An extended repayment period is permitted for loans for the purchase or improvement of your principal residence.

•The amount of the loan cannot be larger than (1) $50,000 less your highest outstanding loan balance in the prior 12 months, or (2) half of your vested plan benefits ($10,000 if your vested benefits are under $20,000), whichever is less.

The vested portion of your retirement-plan benefits, which you are borrowing against, *can* be used as security for the loan.

Source: Irving Blackman, partner of Blackman, Kallick & Co., 180 N. LaSalle St., Chicago 60601.

Withdraw Savings from IRA Before 59½, Pay the Penalty, And You're Still Way Ahead

A *deductible* IRA can be a better place to keep your savings than a money fund or regular savings account, even if you plan to use the money before you retire. That's because the tax advantages of a deductible IRA contribution are so great that they can outweigh the penalty that applies when funds are withdrawn from the IRA before age 59½.

Key: IRA contributions are made with pretax dollars. A person in the 38.5% bracket who earns an extra $1,000 has only $615 to invest after paying taxes. But the *entire* $1,000 can be put in an IRA and be ready to earn even more tax-free interest.

Thus, for an individual in the 28% tax bracket, an investment in a deductible IRA earning 8% interest would be superior to a taxable investment earning the same 8%, in spite of the IRA's early-withdrawal penalty, if the money is left in the IRA for eight years. (If you are in a higher tax bracket for any reason or the IRA earns more than 8%, the break-even point would be less than eight years.)

Source: Jill A. Harris, CFA, Arthur Young & Co., 277 Park Ave., New York 10172.

The 10 Best Places To Retire to in the US

Using six criteria—money matters, climate, personal safety, services, housing, and leisure living—and averaging out the scores of 131 different areas, the highest-ranking places to retire to are:

1. Murray, Kentucky
2. Clayton, Georgia
3. Hot Springs, Arkansas
4. Grand Lake, Oklahoma
5. Fayetteville, Arkansas
6. St. George, Utah
7. Brownsville, Texas
8. Bloomington, Indiana
9. San Antonio, Texas
10. Port Angeles, Washington

Source: *Retirement Places Rated: All You Need to Plan Your Retirement* by Richard Boyer & David Savageau, Prentice-Hall.

Retirement Savvy

The best retirement—or second—careers are those that service businesses in expanding fields and capitalize on your experience, network, and knowledge. You may have to invent the service yourself, but the fields that are most likely to need you are finance (particularly in financial centers), computers, engineering (particularly environmental, electrical, and electronic), management consulting, legal services (particularly corporate bankruptcy, taxation, and international trade), health services (administration), education, medical sales, food services, human resources management, foreign trade, and public relations.

Source: John O. Whitney, professor at Columbia University's Graduate School of Business, and other economists quoted in *New Choices*, 28 W. 23 St., New York 10010.

Cars

Car Owner's Guide To Saving Money

•Buy bargain tires marked *blems.* They are perfectly serviceable except for minor cosmetic blemishes on sidewalls.

•Lengthen the life of old windshield-wiper blades by rubbing the edges with a knife or the striking part of a matchbook cover. This exposes the softer material underneath and improves the wiping ability of the blades.

•Preserve the car's finish by washing it with cold or lukewarm water. But never wash the finish with hot water.

•Run the air conditioner for at least 10 minutes every week. This procedure will maintain coolant pressure and avoid costly air-conditioner breakdowns.

•When you stop for service, get out of the car and watch gas-station attendants carefully, particularly if you have an out-of-state license. When the oil is checked, make sure the dipstick is inserted all the way. Some attendants may show you a dipstick that indicates the oil is low, then use an empty can and pretend to add a quart of oil.

•Clean corrosion off the battery terminals. Use a wire brush or steel wool to scrape battery posts and cable clamps. Clean the top surface with a mild solution of baking soda and water. Don't let the solution seep under cell caps.

•Prevent wind resistance, which cuts performance up to five miles per gallon, by keeping the car windows closed while driving.

•Be aware that every five miles per hour over 50 cuts fuel performance by two miles per gallon.

Good sign: A mechanic certified by the National Institute of Auto Service Excellence, particularly in the system you need repaired.

Source: *Money,* Rockefeller Center, New York 10020.

Choosing a Mechanic

Before the mechanic replaces your alternator, make sure he checks its belt. It could mean the difference between a $200 job and a $20 part.

Right and Wrong Jumper Cables

Car jumper cables that work from cigarette lighter to cigarette lighter aren't effective. The wires can't carry enough amps to do an efficient job, particularly in cold weather, when it takes more power to get a car started. Under optimal conditions—with the battery just below charge and the outside temperature moderate—it can take 10–15 minutes to get your battery working. *Better:* Old-fashioned jumper cables that connect battery to battery. Used properly, they're safer, more efficient, and much faster than the others.

Source: Tony Assenza, racing-car buff and the editor of *Motor Trend,* 8490 Sunset Blvd., Los Angeles 90067.

Rustproofing Scams

Dealer-applied rustproofing should be done as soon as you buy the car. But be *careful.* Read the fine print. Most "guarantees" give you only the cost of rustproofing in case of rust. Make sure the guarantee states that the dealer will repair or replace rusted body panels.

Some rustproofers demand that you return every year at a *strictly specified time* in order to keep the guarantee in effect. They'll usually hit you with a $25 refresher-application bill. Find a rustproofer who will give you at least a month's leeway on that return date.

Rip-off artists simply drill the holes and put in a plastic plug, never applying the rustproofing agent at all. When you get the car home, take off the plugs and insert a screwdriver into the holes. The agent, still a little runny, will come off on the screwdriver. If it's not there, get your money back.

You can save money with a do-it-yourself rustproofing kit. You'll probably do a more conscientious job than a mechanic, anyway, and the materials are equal in quality.

What Car-Rental Agencies Don't Tell You

•*Automatic drop-off can be a rip-off on late-night rental-car returns.* Unlike normal rental-car check-ins, where the clerk totals up the costs and gives you a copy of the bill, automatic drop-offs require you to return all copies. You often don't get a copy until your credit-card company has billed you. *Protection alternatives:* Return your rental car during business hours. Make a copy of the rental form before returning it, noting your entry of the final mileage. Don't pay your credit-card bill *until* you get the car-rental bill and make sure their figures agree with yours. If they have overcharged you, dispute the bill and let the credit-card company know about the problem.

•*Pay traffic tickets you get when driving a rented car.* Many rental companies give the police your name, address, and *home state* license number if you get a ticket. You risk being picked up as a scofflaw back home.

•*Don't pay for more insurance than you need on a rented car.* Rental agents routinely encourage customers to pay around $5 a day for optional collision coverage. Chances are, however, that your own personal-car policy may extend coverage to a rented car. Check the insurance policy before signing up for unnecessary coverage.

•*Be wary if the car-rental agency asks for the name of your auto insurance company.* Chances are they're giving you only *secondary* liability insurance coverage. That means *their* insurance company won't pay until your own insurance is exhausted (and your own premiums will go up).

•*Give a rental car the once-over before driving away in it.* Check the headlights, turn signals, and brakes. Squirt the windshield washer to be sure there is water. Check the oil level. Drive it around the block before taking it onto the expressway.

Best Ways to Protect Your Car from Thieves

A quality security device installed on your car will more than pay for itself on insurance-premium savings alone.

Many insurance companies provide premium discounts for cars with antitheft systems.

One of the best ways to reduce premiums is by increasing the deductible on your insurance policy. A good antitheft device will help cut premium costs by increasing your deductible—while reducing the risk that you will ever have to pay it.

Antitheft basics: You want the car thief to know that you do have a security device on your car. Therefore, make sure you let your system show—the little red light under the dashboard is an excellent deterrent—also, you should put a sticker advertising the alarm system in a window.

But you also want to make it difficult for the thief to figure out what he/she has to do to beat your system—and give him very little time to do it.

Trap: Thieves are very familiar with the most popular security systems, such as those installed on new cars at the factory, and can defeat them quickly.

Self-defense: Start by hardening your car's "soft spots." Thieves know the vulnerable spots on your car better than you do. *Example:* Many GM cars are stolen by "peeling" the steering-column casing, a technique used to expose a little rod that can then be moved almost as easily as a key to start the engine. If your GM car has a plastic steering-column casing or one made of lightweight metal, buy a reinforced collar—either one that you have to remove every time you start the car or one that is permanently installed.

Some simple security steps that work:

When you park against a curb, turn the front wheels sharply to the right—or left—and make sure the front of the car is not pointed outward, which would make it too easy to tow away. The thief would then have to tow the car from the rear—and won't because the angle of the front wheels makes the car almost impossible to control.

Buy a car alarm that sounds when a car is tilted, again to defeat towing.

Have all the windows and major parts (doors, fenders, bumpers, tops, and fancy wheels) etched with the car's vehicle identification number (VIN). Body shops that know they are subject to search by the police won't accept parts that are marked this way—and thieves know that. *Most effective:* Put a sign in the window noting that the parts have all been marked.

Install a toggle switch (cost: less than $5) on the wire that runs from the ignition to the starter and hide it amid the wires under the dash or run it under a car seat. Turn the switch off when you leave the car. *Catch:* Read the warranty on a new car first. Some manufacturers make it difficult to buy anything but a dealer-installed system by voiding the warranty on the car's electrical system if a wire is cut to install a security device.

Source: Ken MacKenzie, investigator with the Richardson, Texas, police department and an officer of the International Association of Auto Theft Investigators, 255 S. Vernon, Dearborn, MI 48124. Barnet Fagel is first vice president of the Vehicle Security Association, 2101 L St. NW, Washington, DC 20037, and public safety liaison manager, International Teletrac Systems, 9800 La Cienega Blvd., Inglewood, CA 90301.

Real Estate

When Buying a New Condominium

Before signing any contract for a new condominium, which is harder to check out than an established condominium, buyers should study the prospectus for any of these pitfalls:

The prospectus includes a plan of the unit you are buying, showing rooms of specific dimensions. But the plan omits closet space. *Result:* The living space you are buying is probably smaller than you think.

The prospectus includes this clause: The interior design shall be substantially similar. *Result:* The developer can alter both the size and design of your unit.

The common charges set forth in the prospectus are unrealistically low. Buyers should never rely on a developer's estimate of common charges. *Instead:* They should find out the charges at similarly functioning condominiums.

Common charges include: Electricity for hallways and outside areas, water, cleaning, garbage disposal, insurance for common areas, pool maintenance, groundskeeping, legal and accounting fees, reserves for future repairs.

Variation on the common-charge trap: The developer is paying common charges on unsold units. But these charges are unrealistically low. *Reason:* The developer has either underinsured, underestimated the taxes due, omitted security expenses, or failed to set up a reserve fund.

The prospectus includes this clause: The seller will not be obligated to pay monthly charges for unsold units. *Result:* The owners of a partially occupied condominium have to pay for all operating expenses.

The prospectus warns about the seller's limited liability. But an unsuspecting buyer may still purchase a condominium unit on which back monthly charges are due, or even one on which there's a lien for failure to pay back carrying charges.

The prospectus makes no mention of parking spaces. *Result:* You must lease from the developer.

The prospectus is imprecise about the total number of units to be built. *Result:* Facilities are inadequate for the number of residents.

The prospectus includes this clause: Transfer of ownership (of the common property from the developer to the homeowners' association) will take place 60 days after the last unit is sold. *Trap:* The developer deliberately does not sell one unit, continues to manage the condominium, and awards sweetheart maintenance and operating contracts to his subcontractors.

The prospectus specifies that the developer will become the property manager of the functioning condominium. But the language used to spell out monthly common charges and management fees is imprecise. *Result:* The owners cannot control monthly charges and fees.

Source: Dorothy Tymon, author, *The Condominium: A Guide for the Alert Buyer*, Golden-Lee Books, Brooklyn, NY.

Traps in Homeowner's Insurance

Many home buyers hastily purchase homeowner's insurance to qualify for their mortgage. *Problem:* They don't understand the choices involved in insuring a home.

Basic insurance: If a fire or other catastrophe destroys your home, you get the replacement cost, which is enough to rebuild the home to its original state. You carry at least 80% of the replacement cost. *What you don't get:* The market value of the home so that you can go out and buy a similar one. Land value and neighborhood are inherent in market value, yet unrelated to replacement cost.

Carry at least 80% of the home's replacement value. If you don't, the insurance company penalizes you by the percentage you underinsure.

Example: You have a $100,000 house and carry only $60,000 on it. That is three quarters of the $80,000 required. If you have $20,000 worth of damage from a fire, you will get only $15,000, or three quarters of your damage. If you were insured for $80,000, you would get full coverage.

How to ascertain replacement cost:

Most insurance companies will inspect your house if it is worth more than $100,000.

Your broker has a replacement-cost guide. This determines the cost of the average home by computing the number of rooms and square feet. It is an educated guess.

If your home was custom-built, get an independent appraisal.

Replacement cost versus actual cash value: Replacement cost is only useful when you rebuild your house. If you decide to walk away and buy another house, you will get only the actual cash value. *What it is:* replacement value minus depreciation.

Example: You have a 50-year-old home worth $100,000 and $80,000 worth of insurance. You might get only $40,000 if you decide not to build, because depreciation could take away as much as 50% of the payment. (Depreciation computed by an insurance company is not related to depreciation for tax purposes. Depreciation is rarely in excess of 50% of a home.)

Inflation protection: Most insurance companies automatically increase coverage by whatever it costs to rebuild a home in your area. This automatic increase has been running about 10%.

Check out: Whether inflation increases are granted annually, semiannually, or quarterly. *Problem:* If inflation is running 10% and you have a disaster after six months, you may have insufficient coverage. *Best:* Ask for an endorsement that increases protection quarterly. It costs little. Some insurers don't charge for it.

Other coverage included in a homeowner's policy:

The cost of staying in a hotel or renting a temporary apartment or house while your own home is repaired. *Coverage:* Up to 20% of insurance of the home's contents (furniture, china, clothing, etc.). *Coverage:* Fifty percent of the insured value of the house.

Third-party liability: Protection in case anyone is injured on your property. *Example:* A party guest slips on a rug and breaks an anklebone. *Or:* Someone is injured through some action of yours off your property. *Example:* You hit someone with a golf ball.

Appurtenant structures: A garage or shed. *Coverage:* 10% of home coverage.

Theft away from home: This covers a suitcase stolen from your locked car, etc. *Caution:* This coverage is limited and optional in some states.

Examine policies for restricted coverage on jewelry, furs, silverware, fine art, money, and securities. Schedule high-value items so that you and the insurer agree on their value before there is a loss.

Keep accurate records of your possessions. Don't keep the records where they can be destroyed with the rest of your home.

Seek the broadest coverage possible within your budget. Some homeowners' policies are little more than fire-insurance contracts. *Caution:* No homeowner's policy covers floods. Flood coverage must be obtained separately. The best policies, known as all-risk policies, cover nearly everything and take the burden of proof of coverage away from you. They make the insurance company prove it is excluded from the contract.

Example: A deer jumped through a picture window and tore through the house. The entire interior was destroyed, since the deer either broke or bled on nearly everything. A standard policy would not cover this incident. Under an all-risk policy, the company must pay unless it can prove that the incident falls within a specific exclusion from coverage set out in the policy.

Look for credits for higher deductibles, particularly percentage deductibles.

Example: You insure your house for $100,000. Instead of getting a $500 deductible, you can get a credit for a 1/2% deductible. However, realize that when the amount of the insurance is raised 10% the next year, your deductible will rise proportionately—from $500 to $550.

Look for credits for burglar and fire alarms.

Look into companies that pay dividends.

Source: Judith L. Robinson, CPCU, vice president of general insurance brokers, H&R Phillips, 622 Third Ave., New York 10017.

Figures to Check at Real Estate Closing

Monthly payments.

Per diem figures for utilities, taxes, and/or interest.

The broker's commission.

The rent, security deposits, and/or interest on deposits that have not yet been transferred.

A charge for utility bills that have already been paid.

A charge for loan fees that have already been paid.

A contractor, attorney, appraiser, or some other party to the contract who has not yet been paid.

How to Minimize Flood Damage

Flooded basements can be good. If a flood reaches your property, water inside will equalize underground pressure outside and prevent collapse of basement walls. Don't pump out the basement until the flood recedes.

If you have no second floor: Remember, water inside a building often gets no higher than two or three feet. Use high shelves for valuables (including the furnace motor).

Keep underground fuel tank full. Otherwise, it can buoy up to the surface, causing foundation walls to collapse. (If no fuel is available, fill the tank with water.)

Reducing Real Estate Tax by Challenging Assessments

Effective real estate tax is tax rate multiplied by *assessed value*. There is not much an individual can do about tax rate, but assessment can often be challenged successfully. *Requirements:* The owner must show either that the property is overvalued or that assessment is higher than on comparable property in the same area.

When to ask for reduction:

•Just before making necessary repairs of damages or deterioration that has lowered the value of the property.

•Local tax records err in description by overstating size or income.

•Net income drops due to factors beyond the owner's control.

•When the price paid for building in an arm's-length transaction is lower than the assessed value.

What to do:

•Determine the *ratio* of the assessed value to the present market value. Compare this with the average ratios of similar properties recently sold in the same area. *Sources:* Ratios available to the public in tax districts. Real estate brokers and professional assessors can also be consulted.

•Check tax records for a description of property and income.

•Consult a lawyer on the strength of the case, whether it can be handled by informal talk with the assessor, how much it will cost if formal proceeding or an appeal is necessary.

Screening Potential Real Estate Investments

Rules of thumb can be dangerous if relied on exclusively for real estate investments, but they do offer a quick and simple way to screen properties. *Two rules:* (1) Don't pay more than 6–7 times the gross annual rent, or 10 times the net operating income, unless the going rate in the area is consistently higher. (2) Think twice if operating expenses eat up from 50% to 70% of gross rentals in an apartment building (leaving 30% to 50% gross income), depending on the geographic area. Major costs include vacancy and collection losses, repairs and maintenance, management fees, heating oil or gas, before deducting taxes and mortgage payments.

Caution: In-depth analysis of the area and property, plus expert legal and real estate advice, is still a must before a final decision is made.

How Real Estate Investors Get Tricked

The urge to invest in real estate, which is still strong in most parts of the country, exposes buyers to sharp practices by sellers.

The most common distortion is a claim of high-paying tenants. If the rent roll of a commercial building shows that nine tenants pay $6–$8 per square foot and three pay $12, find out who the high-paying tenants are. One may be the building owner, and the others may be affiliated with the seller.

Any fudging of current and future income can cost an investor tens of thousands of dollars. In a small building, where the seller reports that 10 tenants pay $400 a month ($48,000 a year), if buildings in the area sell for six times gross, the market price would be $288,000. But suppose the owner had prepared to sell the building by raising the rents from $350 to $400 a month. That increase in the rent roll cost the buyer $36,000 (the difference between six times $48,000 in annual rents and six times $42,000).

Even worse would be the effect on future rent increases. If the rents in the building were close to market before the increase, the owner may well have offered tenants a free month's rent or a delayed increase. A delayed increase means that the buyer will not realize as much income as forecast. A free month's rent means that the actual increase in rents was only $17 an apartment, not $50. If the new owner tries to increase rents well above that, tenants may move.

Other seller claims that buyers must investigate:

•Low operating expenses. Sellers may be operating the building themselves to avoid a management fee. If buyers cannot take care of the building personally, this fee must be added to real operating expenses. And if sellers do not factor it in, the bank will when it calculates the maximum supportable mortgage.

•Reasonable property tax. If the building has not been assessed for several years, the buyer may have a substantial tax bite on the next reassessment. Also, the seller may have made an addition to the building that has not yet been recorded with the tax assessor. As a precaution, ask the local assessment office for a tax card or listing sheet. It will show the building's assessment and indicate when it was assessed. If it was assessed a year and a half ago and there have been no significant structural additions, reassessment may not hurt the buyer. But if it has not been assessed for eight years, there could be a significant tax boost.

While checking the tax card or listing sheet,

check the owner's property description against the one listed. If the owner says that 20,000 square feet are being sold but the tax card says 15,000 square feet, there has been some addition to the structure that has not been recorded and therefore has not been assessed. Or, there may be an assessment error that, when corrected, will raise costs.

•Low insurance premiums. Is coverage in line with the structure's current value? What does the policy cover? Ask to see the policy. Ask an insurance adviser how much more proper coverage will cost if coverage is insufficient.

•Energy-efficient. Verify the owner's claim with the local utility company to determine actual energy costs. Also check with regulatory commissions to see whether utility companies are scheduled to increase their tariffs.

•A real buy. Check the income statement with those of comparable buildings in the area. Consult the annual income and expense analysis by geographical area and building type with the Institute of Real Estate Management (430 N. Michigan Ave., Chicago 60611).

Source: Thomas L. O'Dea, O'Dea & Co., Inc., 2150 Country Club Rd., Winston-Salem, NC 27103.

Tips for Sellers on Selecting a Real Estate Agent

•Avoid the trap of listing property with a relative or friend in the real estate business. Seek out an experienced, full-time agent, preferably one who *specializes* in your type of property or neighborhood.

•Watch out for *supersalespeople*. They often push *easy* properties. If you feel uncomfortable with the agent, or there's some hangup about the property, *find someone else.*

•The real estate office is important, too. It should be attractive, easily accessible, and open seven days a week for residential business. The agency should be a member of a multiple-listing service and be well regarded by financing sources. *Note:* Try to speak with the head of the firm. If you call in cold, you will get and be stuck with the broker who is on duty that day.

Ways of Listing Property for Sale

•*Open listing:* The owner reserves the right to sell the property himself/herself or to retain brokers.

•*Exclusive agency:* No other broker will be hired as long as the original broker is retained (usually for a specified period), but this doesn't prevent the owner from selling the property himself.

•*Exclusive right to sell:* The broker gets his commission when the property is sold, whether by the broker, the owner, or anyone else.

•*Multiple listing:* Brokers combine to sell properties listed with any member of the brokers' pool. The brokers themselves split commissions between the listing and selling broker.

If no time is specified, the listing is good for a "reasonable" time. The owner can revoke the listing at any time before the broker has earned his commission, provided he acts in good faith and doesn't revoke it when negotiations have been substantially completed.

If a time is specified, the agreement will end as stipulated. It would continue only if the owner has waived the time limit by accepting the services of the broker, or if the owner has acted in bad faith (as by postponing agreement with a buyer until after the time limit). In some states, if the listing is for a specified time, the owner can revoke the listing only up until the time the broker has put money and effort into the listing contract.

If nothing is said, the broker will earn his commission on finding a buyer who is ready, willing, and able to buy on the terms specified. The owner, to protect himself, should ask for a provision under which payment of the commission will depend on closing the deal and on receiving full payment.

Selling Your House When Credit Is Tight

When mortgage rates are high, homeowners can entice buyers with offers to finance the sale themselves. By offering financing, sellers may make their house so marketable that outside financing will be unnecessary. And the commission saving is substantial.

However, although financing the sale of a house is simple in principle, sellers should have the advice of a lawyer who specializes in real estate.

Four basic methods:

•First mortgage. If you are trying to sell a $100,000 house that has no mortgage (a rarity) and the purchaser can afford only $40,000 cash down, then the purchaser simply gives you a first mortgage for $60,000, which is paid out over an agreed-upon period at an agreed-upon interest rate. In case of default, you keep the cash and foreclose on the house.

•Second mortgage. If you are trying to sell the

same $100,000 house with an existing $50,000 first mortgage, a second mortgage reduces the cash that a buyer would need. The purchaser assumes the first mortgage and gives you a $20,000 down payment. The purchaser then gives you a second mortgage for $30,000. Interest rate and maturity date are negotiable. But many existing first mortgages held by institutional lenders contain a due-on-sale clause, which prohibits the sale of the house without the consent of the lender. Typically, such consent is given only if the interest rate is increased substantially.

•Wraparound. Similar to second mortgages. Using the same numbers as in the second-mortgage example, you get a $20,000 down payment, but instead of taking back a $30,000 second mortgage, you take back an $80,000 wraparound mortgage (the amount of the first mortgage plus the remaining $30,000 of the sales price). One advantage is that defaults are quick to catch because the buyer makes all payments directly to you and you pay the first-mortgage portion to the lender. Another advantage is that the interest rate on the wraparound is calculated on the entire $80,000, even though the $50,000 first-mortgage portion may be at a lower interest rate. Therefore, you receive the interest average, giving you a higher yield on your $30,000 portion.

•Leasing with purchase option. Lease payments may be applied to the purchase price, an amount agreed on when the deal is made. The best approach is to make the term as short as possible. If another prospective buyer comes along with ready cash, you won't be hindered by a long-term contract. And since you are still the owner, you can depreciate the house as a rental unit.

Source: C. Gray Bethea, Jr., vice president and general counsel, CMEI, Inc., Atlanta.

Estate Planning

How Much Life Insurance You Need

First step: Determine what the surviving members' short- and long-term economic needs are likely to be. Then, estimate the amount of these needs covered by available resources (savings, home equity, existing insurance, pension benefits, veterans' benefits, and Social Security). Buy only enough life insurance to make up the deficit between needs and available resources.

How to determine needs:

Immediate cash for death-related expenses. For uninsured medical costs, funeral expenses, debts, taxes, and estate-settlement fees (including the lawyer's bill). Minimum amount of cash: $4,000.

Readjustment fund. Takes economic pressure off the family, allowing them to make important decisions without haste. *Optimum size:* Six to 12 months of the lost net income of a working parent or the one-year cost of replacing the family services of a nonworking parent.

Mortgage funds. Mortgage-canceling life insurance gives survivors relatively low-cost housing (that is, they pay only taxes and upkeep). If they decide to sell the house, insurance relieves the pressure to sell too quickly at a distress price.

Family income. Make two budgets and review them periodically. One budget applies if the father's income is lost. The other applies either to replace a working mother's lost income or the cost of replacing her services at home.

Emergency fund. For an unexpected crisis, such as a major illness. *Amount:* About $2,000 (adjust for the size and health of the family).

Widow's income. Drops in proportion to her decreasing financial responsibility to the children. After the children are on their own, she may not need extra income if she remarries or takes a job. Otherwise, she would need extra income if she does not remarry or work, for Social Security benefits stop when her youngest child turns 18 and will not resume until she reaches 60.

Special funds. To cover the cost of the children's college education, etc.

Some guidelines:

Comparison shop for price and quality of insurance coverage.

Fill short-term needs, such as mortgage protection or supplemental income during the children's early years, with the lowest-cost term insurance available. Fill long-term needs with the least expensive whole-life insurance.

Know your life insurance needs before talking to insurance agents. Don't get pressured into making the wrong purchase.

Useful rule of thumb:

After the death of its principal income producer, a family requires 75% of its former after-tax income to maintain its standard of living, according to a Citibank report. It must, according to the report, have at least 60% to get along at all.

Here is the amount of life insurance (in terms of annual-earnings multiples) needed to provide this income at different ages (taking into account Social Security benefits and assuming the insurance proceeds were invested to produce an after-inflation return of 5% a year, with the entire principal consumed over the survivor's life expectancy).

Present Age	Your Present Earnings $15M	$23.5M	$30M	$40M	$65M
25 years					
75%	4.5	6.5	7.5	7.5	7.5
60%	3.0	4.5	5.0	5.0	5.5
35 years					
75%	6.5	8.0	8.0	8.0	7.5
60%	4.5	5.5	6.0	6.0	6.0
45 years					
75%	8.0	8.5	8.5	8.0	7.5
60%	6.0	6.5	6.5	6.0	6.0
55 years					
75%	7.0	7.5	7.0	7.0	6.5
60%	5.5	5.5	5.5	5.5	5.0

While the chart shows insurance needs, it would be more useful to say that it shows capital requirements. Those requirements can be met by life insurance or through savings and investments, employee benefits, or inheritance. Thus, to the extent that the independent capital resources are built up, insurance needs diminish.

Understanding Term Insurance

Term insurance is usually the least expensive form of insurance coverage you can get for a maximum of five years.

The choices:

Yearly renewable term. The rates start low and rise annually as your age (which increases the risk) goes up. Choose this policy if you're in a short-term venture (a construction project or a short-term contract).

Five- and 10-year term insurance. Appropriate for a person starting a high-risk or highly leveraged business when the bank may insist that the entrepreneur's life be covered by a large policy for a specified period of time. The premium is averaged out on an annual basis over the life of the policy.

Yearly renewable term policy with a reversion to lower premiums on evidence of insurability. This is a recent development. At a specified time (usually after four or five years), if you pass a medical exam, the premiums can be reduced by perhaps 35% of what they might have been. *Example:* If your insurance premium starts at $1,000 a year and climbs $200 annually, you must pass an exam during the fifth year to get the premium lowered to $1,200. *Potential problem:* Bad health at the time of the examination will negate the possibility of the premium being lowered.

Avoid term insurance even for the short haul if you are almost 70 years old. Since the risk at that age is so high, the point at which term and straight-premium rate crossed would be attained within five years. At that point, a permanent (or straight) life policy would be best.

If you need life insurance for more than five years, permanent insurance is usually best.

Reason: The total acquisition price usually evens out over a period of 10 years. If the buyer is relatively young, say, in his thirties, the cash value of the policy may increase at a greater rate than the premium after the third year. The straight-life policy holder may borrow on the cash value at a tax-deductible, low rate of interest.

Alternative: Some creative insurance agents combine the two types of insurance coverage, thus lowering premium costs and ensuring cash value at a specific time.

Source: Leon Sicular, president, Leon H. Sicular Associates, 350 Fifth Ave., New York 10001.

Tough-Minded Estate Planning

It may seem callous to even think about taxes when a loved one faces a life-threatening illness. But if tax planning is ignored at that point, assets carefully accumulated over a lifetime may be squandered unnecessarily. For many facing a final illness, dealing with these matters provides a life-oriented focus that helps them to combat depression and achieve a sense of completion in seeing that their affairs are well ordered. *Some things to consider:*

•*Gifts by the patient.* In many cases, estate taxes can be saved by making gifts to family members and other intended beneficiaries. An unlimited amount may be transferred tax-free, provided no single person receives more than $10,000. The maximum tax-free gift per recipient can increase to $20,000 if the patient's spouse is still alive and consents to treat each gift as having been made jointly.

Under the old law, gifts made within three years of death were figured back into the taxable estate. The 1981 Tax Act repealed this "contemplation-of-death" rule in most cases. *One major exception:* The old rule still applies to gifts of life insurance.

•*Gifts to the patient.* This tactic may be useful when the patient doesn't have enough property to take full advantage of the estate-tax exemption ($600,000). *Reason:* Property that passes through the decedent's estate gets what's known as a stepped-up basis. That is, the person who inherits it is treated for income tax purposes as though he/she bought it and paid what it was worth on the date of death. (Or what it was worth six months after the date of death if the executor chooses this alternative date to set the value of the taxable estate.)

Example: Mr. Jones, a cancer patient, has $150,000 worth of assets. His wife has a large estate, including $75,000 worth of stock that has a tax basis of $10,000. That means there's $65,000 worth of taxable gain built into the stock. She gives the stock to her husband. (There's no tax on gifts between spouses.) Mr. Jones leaves the stock to the children. The children inherit the stock with the basis stepped up to $75,000. So if they turn right around and sell it for $75,000, there's no taxable gain. With these shares, Mr. Jones's estate is still under $600,000—the exempt amount. So the stepped-up basis is achieved without paying estate tax. And the property is taken out of Mrs. Jones's estate, where it might be taxed.

Caution: In most cases, it doesn't pay to use this tactic with property that will be bequeathed back to a spouse who had given it to the patient. Unless the gift was made more than a year before the date of death, stepped-up basis will be denied. But when the patient is expected to survive for well over a year, this tactic can be quite useful.

Example: Mr. Smith owns a $150,000 rental property with a $25,000 tax basis. Mrs. Smith has a disease that will be fatal within two to five years. She has few assets of her own. So Mr. Smith gives her the building and inherits it back from her a few years later with the basis stepped up to $150,000. This substantially increases his depreciation deductions if he keeps the building and eliminates any taxable gain if he sells it.

•*Loss property:* In general there is a tax disadvantage in inheriting property that is worth less than its original cost. *Reason:* Its tax basis is stepped down to its date-of-death value and the potential loss deduction is forfeited. If the patient has substantial income, it might pay to sell the property and deduct the losses. But it doesn't pay to generate losses that are more than $3,000 in excess of the patient's capital gains. *Reason:* These excess losses can't be deducted currently, and there's likely to be no future year's income on which to deduct them. *Alternative:* Sell the loss property at its current value to a close family member. *Result:* The patient's loss on the sale is nondeductible, because the purchaser is a family member. But any future gains the family member realizes will be nontaxable to the extent of the previously disallowed loss.

•*Charitable gifts.* In some cases, bequests to charitable organizations should be made before death. *Benefit:* Current income tax deductions. But it's important not to give too much away. This tactic may generate more deductions than the patient can use.

•*Flower bonds.* Certain series of US Treasury bonds can be purchased on the open market for substantially less than their full face value, because they pay very low interest. But if a decedent owns these so-called flower bonds on the date of death, they can be credited against the estate tax at their full face value.

Timing: Flower bonds should be bought when death is clearly imminent. There's little point in holding them for substantial periods before death because they yield very little income. On the other hand, it does no good for the estate to purchase them after death because they won't be applied against the estate tax. In some cases, flower bonds have been bought on behalf of a patient in a coma by a relative or trustee who holds a power of attorney. The IRS has attacked these purchases. But the courts have so far sided with the taxpayer.

Naming the Right Executor

Naming a spouse or a grown child as an executor is a touching gesture. And they'll also get to keep the estate's administration fee (which can run to 4% or more of the gross estate). The fee would otherwise go to an outsider.

True, the relative (usually the widow) may not have any specialized knowledge of estate administration, but so what? An experienced lawyer and an accountant can be hired to see things through. You might even supply a few recommended professionals to help when the time comes.

Life—and help—aren't that simple, however. *Point:* The executor is personally responsible for estate-tax liabilities and late filings, as well as for making sure that the estate is distributed in accord with the will. He/she is not relieved of this responsibility by delegating to a lawyer the task of "doing whatever is necessary."

Exception: In a very few cases, courts have waived personal penalties when an executor with no business or tax experience, and with scant formal education, had relied upon a seasoned lawyer to take care of the matter. *Warning:* The great weight of court authority is to the contrary.

An executor also may have to pick up the bill personally if he distributes estate assets to beneficiaries so that there isn't enough left to pay federal taxes. That would happen if there was any reason to suspect that the IRS might still be owed money.

Example: An IRS agent warns the executor that the value of shares in a closely held corporation, as shown on the federal estate-tax return, probably will be jacked up.

The executor may also have been held personally responsible for unpaid taxes if the IRS had not put him on notice that more taxes might be payable.

One case: An executor spoke to an officer of the bank where the decedent had conducted his business. She was informed that the decedent hadn't paid any federal tax on his considerable earnings for years. This should have alerted her to the fact that estate assets couldn't be distributed to heirs without leaving enough for what Uncle Sam would demand. The IRS was paid out of her own funds.

Another liability: An heir can hold the executor personally responsible for the amount the heir may have lost through mismanagement of the estate's assets.

Other problems for a spouse: A spouse, in particular, may be too emotionally upset to do a competent job as executor. That has happened even when the spouse was an attorney with vast estate-tax experience.

A spouse or other close relative is also at a disadvantage in gathering all of the estate's assets as required by law. Relatives and friends may insist that money or property that the decedent had lent to them really had been intended as gifts, with an alleged "understanding" that the advance would be forgotten when the decedent died. A widow would have the unpleasant task of trying to collect from her husband's relatives—or of having to sue them. *A common occurrence in such cases:* The widow instead fails to report assets of that type on the estate tax return, then gets caught by the IRS.

Another danger: An executor might regard her husband's will and its property dispositions as sacrosanct, to be honored at all costs—including the cost to herself.

Example: State laws generally allow a widow a certain percentage of her husband's estate, such as 35%, as dower rights. If he leaves her less, she can "take against the will" and get this 35% at the expense of other beneficiaries. But to preserve family sensitivities, the executor might refuse to tamper with her husband's instructions and therefore would be shortchanging herself.

The saving on administrative fees is not large enough to make that the basis for selecting a family member. An individual is not subject to federal tax on what he/she inherits. But if the widow is the executor, the IRS may claim that part of what she inherited actually had been intended to be payment for administering the estate, and she will be assessed income tax on it.

The other side: Consider the potential expense and other consequences of being an executor. That should help to shape your response if a relative or friend flatters you by inviting you to serve as one. Even if you are offered a fee, it may not be worth it.

When Your Safe-Deposit Box Isn't Safe

It is unwise to keep anything in a safe-deposit box that may be needed quickly when the owner dies. At that time, a bank normally seals the box until legal proceedings (sometimes lengthy) take place.

Don't store:

Original will, cemetery deeds, or burial instructions. (Keep them in a safe place at home or in a vault belonging to your lawyer, executor, or accountant.)

Large amounts of cash. Money in a safe-deposit box is not working for you and suggests intent to evade income tax.

Unregistered property (such as jewelry or bearer bonds) belonging to *someone else.* Courts could presume these items to be your property, and proving otherwise might be difficult.

Store these:

Personal papers, such as birth and marriage certificates, military service or citizenship papers, important family records.

Jewelry, medals, rare coins, stamps, family heirlooms.

Original, signed family or business documents, such as house deeds, mortgage papers, trust agreements, contracts, leases, court decrees.

Securities, registered or bearer.

Final check: Make sure someone knows where the safe-deposit box is and where the key is, too.

Important: Safe-deposit boxes taken out in a corporate name *don't* get sealed upon the death of one of the principals. Might be *very* useful for closely held firms.

Use of Mutual Wills Can Forfeit Marital Deduction

A husband might want to leave a big chunk of property to his wife when he dies, but he may fear that she will make no provision to bequeath any of this property to *his* relatives or friends. She may feel the same way about leaving property to him. One solution to this dilemma is to have the spouses make *mutual wills* in which each party agrees to leave inherited property to the survivor, who after death will leave specified property to designated relatives or friends of both parties.

Problem: The solution may create tax problems involving marital deductions on the estate-tax return. If the wife, for example, was contractually bound by a mutual will to bequeath whatever remains of her late husband's property to, say, the children, his property *has not passed on to her without strings.* This deduction applies only if the property passes outright.

State law is important here to determine whether the property that passes to the widow under her husband's will was really contractually subject to a condition. In one decision on this frequent issue, the court held that under *New York* law, a state resident is bound by such a restriction and hence the property earmarked for the children upon the death didn't qualify for the marital deduction because she didn't receive this property outright and without strings.

Indicated action: Check with a tax counsel for the precedent in your state.

Source: David A. Siegel Estate, 67 T.C., No. 50.

Tax-Free Gifts to Family Save Estate Tax and Income Tax

Annual gifts of up to $10,000 a year per recipient are not subject to gift tax. Married couples can give twice as much. Every year for the rest of your life, you and your spouse can jointly give

$20,000 tax-free to each heir and reduce your taxable estate by the same amount.

Tax savings are impressive even if you're widowed or divorced. An individual with four married children and 10 grandchildren can give the children, their spouses, and their grandchildren $180,000 a year with no tax.

Avoiding tax on gifts of over $10,000: Give a part of the interest each year. Or transfer property through an installment sale, taking back notes that are payable at annual intervals. *You can cancel these notes as they fall due.*

Gifts to reduce family's total income tax: Transfer income-producing assets to low-bracket members. Children can earn up to $1,000 of income from the asset before the parent has to pay income tax in his/her higher tax bracket. (No gift tax if $10,000 limit is observed.)

When Not to Leave Everything to a Spouse

If the estate will be *more than* $600,000, it could be a mistake to leave everything to the widow, even if it reduces or eliminates the estate tax.

Reason: That's only the *first* estate tax. *The second estate tax* will come when the widow dies. If she did not remarry, there would be no marital deduction for her estate.

New York attorney Marvin W. Weinstein, who specializes in taxes and estate planning, suggests using *dual trusts*, in some cases, with one qualified and the other not qualified for the marital deduction. This is important when the objective is to provide liberally for the surviving spouse but reduce estate taxes on transfers to the next generation.

A *marital trust* is eligible for the marital deduction from the estate tax, but the disadvantage is that the assets will be taxed in the wife's estate when she dies.

By contrast, a *nonmarital trust* isn't eligible for the marital deduction from the estate tax. The assets are moved to the next generation without being taxed in the widow's estate when she dies. A typical nonmarital trust would be one in which the widow gets all of the income as long as she lives, but upon her death the principal passes to the children.

The two types of trust differ in the *degree of control* of the assets that the widow has. And there are legal/technical requirements that a good trust lawyer should handle.

These procedures are unnecessary if the estate is less than $600,000, because there's no estate tax below this amount.

Getting Your Money's Worth

Antique Auction Do's and Don't's

•Examine the items at the presale exhibition carefully. (Take along a tape measure and a flashlight.) Beware of wooden furniture with legs made of wood that differs from the surface. Chances are someone has put the piece together from two or more pieces.

•When an item catches your interest, ask the attendant what price it is likely to bring—usually a pretty good estimate.

•If you can narrow your choice to one item of each type, you don't have to attend the auction. Simply decide on the maximum you are willing to pay and place the bid in advance. If a piece isn't bid up to your price, the auctioneer will award it to you at the *next level of bidding*.

Example: If your bid was $250 but the bidding stopped at $175, you will get the piece for $200.

On the other hand, if you cannot narrow your choice to one item of each type and you must be physically present at the auction, find out what time the first item on your list will go on the block. *Rule of thumb:* Most auctions clip along at about 100 items an hour. Hence, if you are planning to bid on Lot 121, you can arrive an hour after the auction is scheduled to begin.

•*Antique* means that an object is 100 years old or older.

•Buyers do best in June, July, August, and December, which are slow months at most auction houses.

•Auctioneers never take anything back. They are not responsible for bidders' errors. When in doubt, take an expert along.

•Don't be overeager. It encourages bids from "phantom" buyers, bidding you up. Best not to open the bidding.

•Don't worry about bidding against dealers. They have to buy low enough to handle their overhead and make a profit.

Best Antiques Shops in NYC

French and English furniture:

•Arthur Ackerman & Sons, 50 E. 57 St., 753-5292.* Stunning collection of 18th-century English furniture. Big selection of Chippendale, Sheraton, and Queen Anne.

•Jean-Paul Beaujard, 209 E. 76 St., 249-3790. Large collection of 19th-century furniture, with emphasis on the French Empire. Some Art Deco.

•Dalva Brothers, 44 E. 57 St., 758-2297. Mainly 18th-century French antiques, but you can also find a few fine Italian and English pieces here.

•Malcolm Franklin, 15 E. 57 St., 308-3344. Fine rare English antiques.

•Kentshire Galleries, 37 E. 12 St., 673-6644. The place for formal English antiques. Eight floors of first-quality English antiques, with the emphasis on Regency.

•Newell Art Galleries, 425 E. 53 St., 758-1970. An eclectic collection of formal furniture and bric-a-brac from Renaissance to Art Deco.

•Florian Papp, 962 Madison Ave., 288-6770. In business since the turn of the century, with three floors of fine 19th-century furniture.

19th-century American furniture:

•Didier Aaron, Inc., 32 E. 67 St., 988-5248.

•Margaret B. Caldwell, 142 E. 82 St., 472-8639.

•Kathy Kurland, 1435 Lexington Ave., 410-4421.

•Don Magner, 309 Henry St., Brooklyn, (718) 624-7296.

Other specialty shops:

•Rita Ford, 19 E. 65 St., 535-6717. Finest collection of music boxes in the city.

•Edwin Jackson, Inc., 307 E. 60th, 759-8210. Antique fireplaces, mantels, and accessories.

•Leo Kaplan Antiques, 967 Madison Ave., 249-6766. Eighteenth-century English pottery, paperweights, etc., and a large selection of French cameo glass.

•Lillian Nassau, 220 E. 57 St., 759-6062. The best place in the US to buy Tiffany glass. Also has a fine collection of Art Nouveau and Art Deco glass and accessories.

•James Robinson, 15 E. 57 St., 752-6166. Antique silver, china and glass, and a fine collection of antique jewelry.

•Minna Rosenblatt, 844 Madison Ave., 288-0250. Tiffany and other antique glass, plus a lovely collection of French cameos.

•Philip Suval, Inc., Box 6011, New York 10022, 517-8293. Incredible collection of antique English porcelain and pottery, paintings, and

*Area code is 212 unless otherwise noted.

porcelains from the China trade. By appointment only.

•A la Vieille Russie, 781 Fifth Ave., 752-1727. Specializes in Imperial Russian Fabergé accessories and jewelry.

For Art Collectors

When to buy art: Year-end is the worst time to buy from a dealer. *Best time:* May and June, when dealers seek to wind down inventory for the end of the business year. In the summer, many dealers travel to Europe on buying trips or go on vacation. They would prefer to have sold most or all of their art before departing. As a result, they are likely to be more receptive to lower offers from collectors than they would otherwise be. Be prepared to pay immediately upon acceptance of an offer.

•Beware of art-print stores and galleries that promise appreciation in value. Over 90% of art sold *depreciates*—quickly.

•Get out of an art field when it hits the front pages. The peak has arrived.

•Stay up to date on the art market by subscribing to *ARTnewsletter* (5 W. 37 St., New York 10018). It gives sale prices—and tells which paintings don't sell.

Stereo Savvy

Reduce tape hiss by recording at a high volume...just short of distortion. Before recording on a new cassette, rewind it once to settle the tape on the spools.

Avoid "rumble" by placing a standard red rubber eraser between the dust cover and the turntable; vibrations will escape instead of feeding back through the needle.

Stereo Speaker Placement

(1) Small speakers can supply a richer bass if moved to the corners of the room. Large speakers may sound too booming if put in corners. (2) Small speakers may give better stereo imaging when raised from the floor. (3) Never face speakers toward a smooth plaster wall or picture window. A hard surface bounces the sound back and makes the music shrill. (4) To be sure the speakers are "in phase," switch to the monaural mode and stand midway between them. Shift your head from side to side. If the sound doesn't seem to come from exactly halfway between the speakers, they're out of phase. *Solution:* Reverse the wires at the rear of *one* speaker.

Buying a Stereo Cabinet

(1) Omit the casters on tall cabinets. They shouldn't be moved when full because they're top-heavy. (2) Look for a hinged glass or an acrylic top to serve as a dust cover for your turntable. (3) Insist on adjustable shelves so you can tailor space to your components. (4) Be sure there are holes in the back panel for ventilation and for threading wires through.

How to Talk to Computer Salespeople

Inexperienced shoppers often feel overwhelmed by technical details when they shop for a personal computer. Some things to know:

Bytes: A byte is a unit of information that may correspond to a letter, number, or special character. A megabyte—the unit in which computer components are typically discussed—contains 1 million bytes.

Processor: The processor is the main element of the computer. It handles all manipulation of data and is the primary component responsible for the computers power/speed performance. Processor speed is usually measured in megahertz (Mz).

Random access memory (RAM): RAM is working electronic "memory," which stores programs and data electronically. This memory is manipulated by the processor. When a program is "loaded," the program is read from a disk storage device into RAM. RAM is emptied when the computer is turned off. RAM can be expanded by adding memory chips and/or memory boards. The amount of RAM necessary is determined by the computer software programs that will be operated.

Disk storage: Both floppy disks and hard drives use a magnetic medium similar to audiocassette tapes to store programs and data electronically. Information saved on disks is retained even if the equipment is turned off. The amount of disk storage is determined by both the computer software programs and the amount of data that will be saved.

Monitors: Monitors are the televisionlike devices on which information is displayed. Monitors can be either black and white or color and come in various levels of resolution and graphics capacity. Monitors are controlled by a monitor-interface board inside the computer. Interface boards can either be built in or plugged into the computer's system board. This is determined by the user's needs.

Expansion: Expansion is the ability of the computer to accept hardware in the form of upgradable processors, additional RAM capability, specialized circuit boards, and additional disk storage space. This is a major factor in keeping the computer from becoming obsolete.

Computer Cautions

•Computer insurance trap. Personal computers kept and used at home *for business* aren't covered by homeowner's insurance. (PCs used only for personal use *are* covered by homeowner's policies.) If the home computer is written off as a business expense, special computer insurance is needed.

•Extended warranties on personal computers make sense only if they cover the printer, keyboard, and disk drive. If the policy covers just the computer, it's probably not worth the investment. *Reason:* A computer's central processing unit has few moving parts. It's the other components that are more likely to break down.

Coaching for College Entrance Exams

Is coaching for the SAT test worth it? Even the lowest estimate cites average gains of 34 points. Some reputable schools are reporting increases of up to 100 points. Reasoning and problem-solving skills *are* coachable. *Before spending the money:* Check out the school. The course should include at least 30–40 hours of in-class instruction spread over 6–12 sessions, small classes, and up-to-date materials. *Coaching is particularly valuable if your son or daughter:* (1) Is a newcomer to the tests, (2) tends to become nervous during exams, (3) chooses a highly selective college.

Buying Kitchen Knives

Stick to blades made from *high-carbon stainless steel.* It's the only material that holds a sharp edge *and* resists rust and stains. Make sure the handle is attached with rivets, *not* adhesive. Never put knives in the dishwasher, no matter what the manufacturer says. Wipe the blade and handle clean and store in a knife rack. Keep knives sharpened. *Dull* blades cause accidents.

How Utility Meters Work

Both electricity and gas meters operate on the same principle. Each has several dials with pointers that tell you how much of the energy source you are using.

Electricity meter:

It has five numbered dials. The pointers on three of the dials turn clockwise while the other two turn counterclockwise.

It is read from left to right. The pointer always registers the number it has just passed. *Example:* If the pointer rests between three and four, read the number as three. This holds true even if the pointer is touching the four but has not gone past it.

The numbers taken off each of the dials gives you the reading of the meter at that moment. When it is read again (usually in a month), you'll know how many kilowatt-hours of electricity have been consumed.

Meters can be wrong. Electricity meters can wear out or be damaged during an electrical storm. A dramatic increase in your electric bill should signal a call to the utility company.

Gas meter: It is read exactly the same way as the electricity meter. *Difference:* It has four dials. The pointers of two turn clockwise while the other two turn counterclockwise.

Insurance Policies You Only *Think* You Need

Avoid special policies for cancer or other diseases and mail-order hospitalization plans. The payout on such plans is typically just 50 cents of each premium dollar—or less.

Credit life insurance. This is a very poor bet unless you are quite old or in poor health.

Auto-rental insurance. Only on an icy night in a strange town when you have had a few drinks might this coverage be worth the price. (*Best:* Don't drive at all.) Otherwise, about $4 of each $5-a-day you pay goes not to insurance but to the rental company's expenses and profits.

Source: Andrew Tobias, the author of *The Invisible Bankers: Everything the Insurance Industry Never Wanted You to Know,* The Linden Press, 1230 Ave. of the Americas, New York 10020.

What Supermarkets Don't Tell You

Supermarkets usually place the most expensive items at eye level, where they are more likely to be selected on impulse. *Recommended:* Look at the entire group of products before deciding on a purchase, unless you have a preference for a specific brand.

Generic items can offer real savings, but quality varies widely. *Best bets:* Products such as household bleach, which, by law, must contain specific ingredients common to all brands. *Trap:* When they're on sale, house brands and national brands may actually be cheaper than generic brands. *Point:* Comparison shop.

Bargaining with a Shopkeeper

Getting a better price can be rewarding economically and psychologically. *How to do it successfully:*

Be discreet. A shopkeeper won't reduce a price if he/she is worried that the special value will be made public.

Confine most bargaining to privately owned shops. However, don't write off supermarkets and department stores. Occasionally, managers of these stores will bargain, especially on slightly damaged merchandise or goods that are older and hard to dispose of.

Make it clear to the shopkeeper that you are a serious shopper who intends to spend money. Select several definite articles and several tentative purchases. Ask the shopkeeper for the total cost before writing the bill. As he completes his tally, begin some tongue-clucking and head-shaking. Then, softly ask the merchant if that price is the best he can do.

If he says it is, bargain by offering to pay in cash. This method usually works only if the purchase price exceeds $100.

If the shopkeeper still refuses to bargain, leave everything on the counter and begin to walk out slowly. This ploy may prompt him to reconsider. However, less hard-core bargainers may wish to buy a few of the items anyway and leave the bargaining at that.

Source: *A Shopping Guide to the Lower East Side* by Ellen Telzer and Sharon Greene, 2 Grace Court, Brooklyn, NY 11201.

Canceled Check Is Proof That Fire Insurance Is Paid for, Right? Wrong

Fire and casualty policies should be in hand (on file) before the full premium is paid. One firm, after finding its plant burned to the ground, didn't have the policy it had paid for. Though it presented the canceled check to the broker, its claim was disallowed. The wise course is to buy insurance as you would an automobile: Give the broker a small deposit, but don't pay up until the policy has been delivered.

Tip-Off That Phone Bill Is Incorrect

Calls listed *without* a time or with the digits missing (5 P.M. instead of 5:00 P.M.) more often than not have been misbilled.

Source: Alan H. Jordan, telemarketing consultant, Wayne, Pa, writing in *The Office*, 1200 Summer St., Stamford, CT 06904.

Mistakes When Filing Insurance Claims

Failure to accurately calculate losses. It's hard to believe, but many people can't accurately determine their losses—whether by damage or theft. *Reason:* They fail to maintain effective accounting and record-retention procedures to document the losses. It's not uncommon to hear of a situation in which a theft loss amounted to $250,000 but the claimant could substantiate only $100,000 of the loss. It's important to plan ahead with your accountant to determine the best procedures for demonstrating what you own in case you have to make a claim.

Overstating the loss. This is a subtle problem. If a claimant purposely overstates the loss to the point where the insurance company could question his integrity, the latter will take a hard line. Generally, if the claimant takes a fair position, the insurer will still bargain over the loss claim but will be more reasonable.

Underestimating the loss. This sounds like a contradiction of the above, but it's not. Immediately after losses are claimed, the adjuster will ask the claimant for an *estimate* of the damage, *not* an accurate, justified number. The insurer requires such a rough estimate, but be wary of providing a number before taking the time to get a reliable estimate. If the adjuster reports a number that's too low and then must go back later to the insurer and restate it much higher, both his credibility and yours are hurt. He looks foolish. Those hurt feelings can make future loss negotiations tricky. So tell the adjuster about any problems you have in coming up with a number.

How to Collect from Insurance Companies

In many situations, you can negotiate successfully with an insurance company *without* retaining a lawyer. It is important to know *when* to negotiate yourself and *how* to negotiate *effectively.*

Where to Start

Your *insurance agent,* if he/she is *not* an employee of the insurer, should be your first line of inquiry. An independent agent is better able to assist in obtaining the full amount to which you are entitled. A good relationship with clients is what keeps him in business.

He will often present your claim, negotiate it, and obtain a satisfactory settlement for you without charge. He's especially valuable on smaller claims. Also, if you do the negotiating yourself, he can be a major source of information and advice.

Should You Hire a Lawyer?

The major deciding factor is economic. On small claims, a lawyer's fee might be prohibitive, but on larger claims you could lose money by negotiating with an insurance company yourself.

In some cases, you might simply pay a flat fee for the attorney's review of your claim. Initial consultation usually provides you with helpful information and assists the attorney in deciding whether or not it will pay for him to take your case.

Other considerations:

•*Subjective factors.* If you don't feel comfortable retaining a lawyer, go it alone.

•*No-fault versus at-fault states.* Negotiating your own claim makes a lot more sense in a no-fault state, where the insurance company is bound by law to reimburse you for your losses. But even in a no-fault state, or if you don't apply in time for all of the benefits to which you were entitled, your claim may not be honored if the forms are presented incorrectly.

•*Language.* Understanding the convoluted terminology used in insurance policies and law is a major stumbling block for the layperson. To negotiate successfully, you must be comfortable with the language.

•*Reputation.* Some insurance companies deal fairly and quickly. Others are notoriously difficult and slow. Ask your insurance agent or a negligence attorney about the company you are dealing with. You may need legal help to negotiate a favorable settlement with a difficult company.

•*Pain and suffering.* When multiples of out-of-pocket expenses are involved due to pain and suffering, it is best to hire a lawyer. Lawyers can point out losses you have not even thought of. Also, the insurance company will take into account what you are saving by not hiring a lawyer and offer you less.

If You Go It Alone

•*Read the policy very carefully.* Pay special attention to exclusions and coverages. Before presenting your claim, take a close look at the policy. Make sure you're presenting it in a way that makes it *evident* that your claim is covered. (If you can't find your policy, the insurer is obligated to give you a copy.)

•*Document everything completely.* It is the *most important* part of an insurance claim. Support *every* aspect of your claim, including doctor bills, receipts for medicines, transportation for medical reasons, and a letter from your employer stating lost wages. *Think of everything.* Witnessing an injury to a loved one may cause compensable emotional trauma. A husband (wife) can recover for the lost services and companionship of his (her) injured spouse.

•*Find out what your claim is worth.* Ask your insurance agent or a negligence lawyer what a reasonable offer would be in your situation.

•*Be prepared to take a discount.* There has to be a motivation for the insurer to settle a claim. One advantage of negotiating without a lawyer is that a quick settlement may be offered to avoid legal expenses. So decide *what amount you are willing to settle for.* The settlement offer will depend on various factors, including clarity, proof of coverage, damages, documentation, how likely you are to prevail at trial, and the caseload of the court in which you would be suing. (Some insurers offer nothing until the trial date.)

Bodily Injury

Claims for bodily injury can be the most complicated and negotiable, especially when based on pain and suffering.

•*In a no-fault state,* you are limited to out-of-pocket expenses in a nonserious injury. This includes lost wages. *In a fault-governed state, you can* negotiate *for more.*

•*Don't miss damages.* Start at the top of your head and go down to your toes, to include *every* part that's been hurt.

•*Photograph your injury.* In addition to medical reports, photos are the best documentation of suffering.

•*Consider every aspect* of your *life that has been affected by your injury.* Include your career, sports, hobbies, future interests, and family relationships.

•*Ask what a lawyer would ask*—at least *twice* the actual expense when there has been no permanent disability. Where liability is clear, the insurance company will be likely to give you what you ask for if it believes you really had difficulties and were out of work for a few weeks. However, where there has been permanent disability, multiples of expenses do not apply. *Example:* Your medical bills for a lost eye might have been only $3,000, but a jury might award you 50 times that amount.

If You Cannot Reach a Settlement

An insurance company has a *fiduciary duty* (a relationship based on trust, like that with your lawyer or stockbroker) to deal with its clients fairly and in good faith. *What to do if you are not treated well:*

If you feel that the company is either unreasonably delaying your claim or acting in bad faith, make a complaint to your state insurance regulatory agency. In most cases, the agency will write a letter to the company.

•If your time is being wasted by the insurance company's bureaucracy, small claims court may be appropriate. Such action will pressure the company into settling with you more quickly on your terms.

•Many states have laws penalizing an insurer for acting in bad faith. If you feel the company has been acting in bad faith, you can initiate a lawsuit and possibly collect multiples of your claim in punitive damages.

Source: Dan Brecher, an attorney at 230 Park Ave., New York 10169. He has extensive experience in negotiating with insurance companies.

When to Sue an Attorney For Malpractice

The legal profession is now entering its own malpractice crisis. The number of suits brought against attorneys by clients is increasing, and the availability of malpractice insurance is decreasing.

Ground rules for considering a suit against your lawyer:

•Where malpractice is charged in connection with litigation, the client must show that the litigation would have ended with a result more favorable to him/her if the attorney hadn't been neglectful.

•Where the attorney fell below the standards of skill and knowledge ordinarily possessed by attorneys under similar circumstances, expert testimony is needed to support the charge. And the standard may be affected by specialization (which raises the standard of care required), custom, and locality. Locality and custom can't lower the standard, but they may be used in defense to show that the procedure or the law involved is unsettled.

Best way to avoid malpractice charges (and costs of a suit):

•Good communication between lawyer and client.

•Avoid creating a situation in which the lawyer has to handle serious matters for personal friends. The tendency is to deal with them on a more casual basis.

•The attorney should give an honest opinion of each case, good or bad. The client shouldn't press him for a guarantee as to the result and for a value on the claim.

•*All* fee arrangements should be in writing.

•The attorney should spell out the scope of his/her responsibilities, including appeals, and a limit should be placed on costs.

•The agreement should provide for periodic payments unless the matter involves a contingency fee or a default in payment for a withdrawal.

How to Pick a Lawyer

Most people don't need a personal lawyer the way they need a family doctor or tax adviser. Lawyers should be used only for specific tasks—sale of property, making a will or probating an estate, starting a business, separation or divorce, etc. Lawyers are also needed in crises—personal injury or wrongful death or loss of liberty.

First rule of lawyer selection: Define your problem. Then decide what kind of lawyer you need—and pick the lawyer. Common but meaningless evaluation criteria:

•Age. Good lawyers and bad lawyers come in all ages.

•Law school. Even top schools graduate bottom-of-the-barrel people.

•Large firm versus small firm. Not particularly relevant in personal matters.

What Really Matters:

•Common sense—which you can judge on the phone and in the initial meeting.

•Discretion. Check references.

•Appropriateness to circumstances. An excellent real-estate lawyer may be a poor choice for matrimonial cases.

Signs of Incompetence

Competence is hard to assess on your own, though reputation is a good guide. Look for signs of incompetence. Beware of...

•A lawyer who cannot manage his/her own affairs. Check references by phone or in person (most people are reluctant to write candidly, so avoid checking references by letter)...ask questions at the initial conference with the prospective lawyer, including whether he has previously handled matters similar to yours...with what result...and at what cost...check out the lawyer's office to see if it is tidy or sloppy... whether the staff appear to be intelligent, and if they are polite or rude.

•Lawyers who try to get too close to you. For instance, don't consider hiring a lawyer who jumps in and volunteers to invest with you in a deal you want evaluated. A legal relationship should remain a professional one, not a personal one. Friendships may develop, but only after the job is done.

•Glib verbal opinions. Get your advice in writing. Such formality is a healthy discipline for you and the lawyer. *Key:* The client sets the style. The lawyer's response to your organized and businesslike manner will be a good gauge of whether he/she is right for you.

Special Considerations

•Criminal cases. These are more common than most people think. Kids smoking pot... spouses shoplifting...driving while intoxicated ...tax audits. Criminal matters must be taken seriously from the start. Lawyer selection is critical. *Recommended:*

•Avoid big names. You don't want publicity. Too often the mere appearance of a big name alerts the local media.

•Be careful about former prosecutors. They know the ropes and the court personnel, but many are gunslingers at heart who love to try cases just for the fun of it. If they had a 50% rate of convictions after trial as prosecutors, they were doing well. Look for the type who appears comfortable with a little sin and is able to negotiate a civil disposition. For first-time offenders accused of minor offenses, a good lawyer should be able to negotiate an adjournment in contemplation of a dismissal. This means that the case will be dropped and all record of the charge removed, based on good behavior during the period of adjournment—say, six months. Failing that, a good lawyer tries to negotiate a plea to some minor offense.

•Tax audits. Use accountants unless you know you are liable to be charged with substantial fraud. IRS special agents, who conduct audits, are always lawyers. They are more relaxed when facing an accountant because good tax accountants work with IRS special agents regularly. A good accountant can often strike a better deal than a feisty lawyer. Good accountants know, too, when they are in over their heads and will tell you when you must get a lawyer, take the Fifth Amendment, or otherwise play hardball. But bear in mind that playing hardball with the government can be very risky...and very expensive.

•Divorce. Use a matrimonial lawyer who understands your background—cultural, economic, and otherwise. In this highly specialized field, identical issues can mean very different things to people with different backgrounds. Make sure that your attorney shares your background—or that he at least understands it thoroughly.

Self-defense when you hire someone: Set up a pay-as-you-go agreement (except in contingency cases). Monthly or quarterly bills are best. Every time you get a bill, ask yourself whether you have gotten fair value for what you are being asked to pay. If not, talk it over with the lawyer.

Since these fees are coming out of your pocket—legal expenses are seldom covered by insurance—it's important that you deal with your lawyer in a businesslike fashion until you are satisfied with the services rendered and the costs.

Source: Robert Beshar, Esq., is a member of the *Boardroom* Panel of Experts who has been a Wall Street lawyer for almost four decades.

How to Get VIP Treatment At the White House

Most people think that the only way they will ever enter the White House is by joining the tourists and waiting on line for hours. That's true, unless you know the system.

•Best bet...

How to be part of a special VIP tour: Contact your representative or senator. But plan. There are only a few of these tickets available at any given time. Give your congressman plenty of warning.

•Long shot...

How to get invited to a special function: Find out who is being entertained or honored at state dinners or celebrations. For information, call the Office of the Press Secretary. If an appropriate event is scheduled, call the Office of Public Liaison and explain who you are and why you should be invited.

Example: Suppose your business exports agricultural machinery. You find out that a Middle Eastern sheikh and his delegation, including his minister of agriculture, are being hosted by the president at a formal dinner. You call the Office of Public Liaison and ask to be invited. Point out that you are an expert in agribusiness, know about the problems of doing business overseas, and can be an asset both in interacting with the guests and in forwarding American interests overseas.

Of course, if you are known as a worker for, or a member of, an organization or cause sponsored by the First Lady, there are other sources of invitations.

Example: If the First Lady is an advocate for battered women and you are involved in establishing shelters for them, try calling the Office of the First Lady. Find out when she will be hosting the next gathering of advocates, and make a case for being invited.

Finally, devoted party workers and important contributors are often rewarded by an invitation—if they ask for one.

State Lottery Winning Strategy

When playing a state lottery, it's a good idea to choose at least one number that's higher than 31. *Reason:* Many lottery players use number combinations based on birthdays, anniversaries, and other dates. Since this group concentrates on such numbers as 31 or lower, a winning combination with one or more higher numbers will probably be shared by fewer people.

Source: Dr. Jim Maxwell, American Mathematics Society.

Effective Threatening

Threats work when they are able to raise the perceived cost of inaction high enough to get an uncooperative person to change his/her tune. *Objective:* To make people believe that satisfying your request will cost them far less than refusing to satisfy your request.

You've called...you've written a letter... you've pleaded with the company—but you've gotten nowhere with your justified complaint. It's time to raise the ante. The bad will of a disappointed customer won't be sufficient to get action from the company.

Write a letter to the president of the company. Be as brief, factual, and unemotional as possible, and include copies of whatever documentation you have that supports your case. At the left margin, under your signature, write the letters *cc* (for carbon copies), and add an impressive list of names:

- Local, state, and federal elected officials
- Federal Trade Commission
- Local, state, and federal departments of consumer affairs
- State attorney general's office
- Local newspapers
- Licensing bodies
- Regulatory agencies
- Trade associations
- Better Business Bureau
- Executives of advertising media that the seller uses

This kind of pressure is usually sufficient to induce a more conciliatory frame of mind. *Real-life examples:* A defective piano and a faulty car engine were replaced with brand-new ones.

Verbal threat: You can often get good results without even putting pen to paper. A telephone call to somebody who has the ability and authority to resolve your problem may be all that's needed. *For best results:* Start out with someone who is just high enough to be able to help you. Don't go to the top right away because you need to leave room for appeals within the company. Managers are a good starting point.

Get the name of an appropriate manager from the company switchboard and find out to whom the manager reports. Open with, "I've had a difficult time reaching somebody who can help me, Mr. Jones. I wonder whether Ms. Smith (Mr. Jones's boss) knows how a good customer is being treated."

Jones now knows that unless you're pleased with the outcome of the conversation, Smith will hear about it. Jones would prefer that Smith not be bothered.

Key: The small element of personal jeopardy. The last thing Jones wants is to have his boss bothered with a matter he should have been able to handle.

Reasoning:

Better to resolve your legitimate complaint at a small cost to the company—not to him—than risk a "black mark" on his record.

Source: Ralph Charell is former chief executive and chief operating officer of his own Wall Street securities firm and a former network television executive. He's also the author of two best-sellers: *How I Turn Ordinary Complaints into Thousands of Dollars,* Stein & Day, Scarborough House, Briarcliff Manor, NY 10501, and *Satisfaction Guaranteed,* Linden Press, 1230 Ave. of the Americas, New York 10020.

Old TV Warning

If you own a set over five years old, have a repairman take out its instant-on features—its special light bulb can explode and cause a fire.

Source: *Kovel's Antiques & Collectibles Price List* 1991 by Ralph Kovel and Terry Kovel, quoted in *1,001 Home Ideas,* 3 Park Ave., New York 10016.

Career Skills

How to Be Better at Math

A surprisingly large number of adults, including many businesspeople, have a secret fear of numbers. When they have to analyze budget figures, or even calculate a restaurant tip, they react with confusion or panic.

Symptoms of adult math anxiety: Going blank when figures are discussed. Blurring together numbers printed on a page. Forgetting basic mathematical procedures.

Typical results: Avoiding tasks or even entire fields of endeavor that depend on math. Buck-passing or stalling on math-dependent decisions. Failing to question suspicious numbers.

To solve the problem: Dispel myths that math is a rigid discipline or that some people just naturally lack mathematical ability. *Reality:* In many cases, approximate figures will do. Even those not well schooled in math can catch up quickly with proper instruction.

Recommended:

•Always write down figures when they come up in discussions.

•Ask questions if something is unclear. (If others are silent, chances are they are confused, too.)

•Estimate and round off numbers whenever possible.

Work on math problems alone whenever possible. Review the basics that are vital in business: decimals, fractions, and percentages. A good review book is *Quick Arithmetic,* by R. A. and M. J. Carman (John Wiley & Sons).

Especially useful for the math-anxious: *Overcoming Math Anxiety,* by Shelia Tobias (Houghton Mifflin) and *Mind Over Math,* by Dr. Stanley Kogelman and Dr. Joseph Warren (McGraw-Hill).

Source: Dr. Stanley Kogelman, director, Mind Over Math, treatment service, Bayside, NY, and Bonnie Donady, counselor, Wesleyan University Mathematics Clinic, Middletown, CT.

Sounding Better on the Phone

•You can make a better impression on the phone by opening your mouth wider as you speak and moving your lips more. Most people don't move their lips enough, which flattens the tone of their voice. Do not squeeze the phone between your neck and shoulder. This tenses your throat and makes you talk from one side of your mouth.

•Speak in your lower vocal range. Telephones transmit lower pitches more truly than higher tones.

Time-Savers

To get off the phone fast, get a clue to the other person's activity *early* in the conversation and use it to *close. Example:* "Did I interrupt you?" might bring the response "No. Just going over some budget figures." Then conversation can be ended with, "Okay, I'll let you get back to your budget."

•When calling a long-winded party, time the call for just before he goes out to lunch or leaves for the day. Give *him* a reason to keep the call short without offending him.

•When asking someone to call back later, suggest the best time to call. Avoids repeated interruptions at inconvenient moments.

•Never hold the phone while waiting for someone who's on another line. Request an immediate callback instead.

•Make phone calls before 9 A.M. or after 3 P.M. At other hours, too many people are in meetings.

•Don't return all calls the minute you get back to the office. Spot the crucial ones. Half of the rest will be from people who've already solved their problems; the rest will get back to you soon enough.

•Use a time-reminder device to limit the length of conversations. (Often "politically" desirable to look annoyed when it goes off.)

•Set some appointments at odd times instead of on the hour or half hour. Meeting at 2:50 or 3:20 makes others more prompt and puts across the message of careful time management.

•Accumulate quick, easy, yes/no work in a special "children's hour." Set aside odd periods to work on it (while waiting for a meeting to start, while waiting in the airport, while riding on a commuter train).

•To find your coat fast on a crowded rack. Tuck one sleeve over a hanger bar. To spot your car quickly in a crowded parking lot, mark the antenna with brightly colored tape.

Getting Ready for a Job Interview

A job interview is like a game. It has rules, and the participants have roles to play. What you can win is an offer. What the interviewer can win is the proper person for the job.

Your role as interviewee is to play the confident applicant who can project talent, willingness, and suitability for the opening. If you have done your homework, you should have no problem. *What to do:*

•Spend the morning in the library researching the company, or talk to friends who know similar organizations.

•Interview yourself on a tape recorder until you hear confidence in your answers to questions.

•Prepare positive answers to such potentially difficult queries as "I'm a little worried about your lack of experience" or "You've been out of work a long time, haven't you?"

Interviewers play one of four general roles:

•The target-directed interviewer is direct, businesslike, and a little impersonal. Respond in kind.

•The all-in-the-family interviewer is warm, friendly, and company oriented. Emphasize your team-player attributes.

•The thinking person's interviewer is interested in how you did things or intend to do things. Give logical, expanded answers about your methods and theories.

•The make-it-easy-for-me interviewer is unpredictable and prone to snap judgments. Be a responsive audience, and let the interviewer keep center stage.

Source: Robert Half, president, Robert Half International, Inc., New York, and author of *The Robert Half Way to Get Hired in Today's Job Market,* Rawson Wade.

Talking Salary

Guidelines for salary negotiations when job discussions get down to the nitty-gritty:

•Try not to specify a figure. (It will inevitably be lowered.) Get the other person to mention one first.

•Evade the question. If you are asked what you made at your last job, say: *That salary is not especially relevant because the job I was doing was very different from what I'll be doing now. Perhaps if you could tell me what the salary range is, I could say whether it seems appropriate.*

•Ask for the salary range of workers reporting to you if the company has no established salary range.

•Establish the value of benefits before agreeing on a salary figure.

•Ask for a performance and salary review in six months.

What to Leave Out Of Your Résumé

The style used for writing résumés has changed over the past few years to make them more persuasive and concise. *Goal:* Each résumé entry should persuade readers that they should hire the writer.

What to omit:

Photos. A picture may give employers misleading impressions.

Salary requirement. Why should applicants price themselves out of a job or show that they are a bargain?

Reasons for leaving jobs. These are better explained in interviews.

Date of résumé preparation or date available to begin work. Both indicate how long you have been looking for a job. *Exception:* When you're looking for seasonal work.

References or a statement that references are available on request. *Instead:* List them on a separate sheet and adapt them to each employment situation.

Empty assurances. All applicants think they are good, honest, loyal, and healthy workers. Demonstrate these qualities through concrete examples during interviews.

Vague references to time gaps. Employers look for holes. Explain them in terms of accomplishments. *Example:* Travel to improve a language capability or research a specific project. *Caution:* Never claim to have been a consultant without proof.

Hobbies and outside interests. *Exceptions:* Those that relate to professional interests or show traits that an employer wants. Avoid listing any dangerous or time-consuming activities.

Source: *Résumés: The Nitty-Gritty* by Joyce Lain Kennedy, Suburban Features Inc., Cardiff, CA.

Healthy Sex Secrets

How to Buy Sperm

People considering artificial insemination should be wary of sperm banks. Many of them are popping up across the country, and some have not been approved by state health departments. Protection...

•Call your local health department and ask if the sperm bank has been approved by the state's health department.

•Ask for proof that a sperm donor has been retested for the HIV virus six months after giving the sperm...and ask to see a copy of a permit, license, or letter of approval from the state health department indicating that the sperm bank tests semen or donors for hepatitis B, sexually transmitted diseases, blood group and RH, and other genetically transmitted diseases.

•Inquire about the donor's sperm count. It should be 30–50 million sperm per milliliter in order to increase the odds of successful insemination.

Source: Dr. Jeanne Linden, MD, director of the blood and tissue resources for New York State's Health Department.

Exercise: The Real Aphrodisiac?

Researchers and common sense have long held that exercise enhances health and makes people feel better about themselves and their bodies. This, in turn, makes them more sexually attractive and responsive. Now studies are suggesting that exercise is a potent stimulus to hormone production in both men and women. It may, in fact, chemically increase basic libido by stepping up the levels of such hormones as testosterone.

Source: Whole Body Healing by Carl Lowe, Rodale Press, Emmaus, PA.

Contraceptive Update

New intrauterine devices (IUDs) are small. Some are impregnated with minute amounts of copper and progesterone to enhance efficiency. But they can still cause side effects, some serious.

Examples: cramping, pelvic infection, and painful intercourse. Women who want children later in life are discouraged from using IUDs because in some cases they can lead to sterility.

Source: International Fertility Research Program, Research Triangle Park, NC 27709, and the National Center for Health Statistics, 3700 East West Highway, Hyattsville, MD 20782.

Sex Before Exercise Myth

If you exercise, you've probably heard the myth that sex before an athletic event leads to poor performance.

Fact: At worst, sex before strenuous physical activity has no effect on performance. At best, it may improve performance due to the sense of well-being it produces.

When Condoms Prevent Disease And When They Don't

Condoms offer protection against some venereal diseases (gonorrhea, nongonococcal urethritis, and yeast infections). They are less effective against herpes, venereal warts, and chlamydia, which are small enough to pass through the pores of the condom. If either partner has an active urethral infection or genital lesion, the only safe course is sexual abstinence.

Source: Dr. Michael Carrera, professor of health sciences, Hunter College School of Health Sciences, City University of NY.

Best Time for Older Men to Have Sex

Older men who have trouble attaining erections at night can do better with morning sex. Testosterone levels are higher earlier in the day.

Source: Medical Aspects of Human Sexuality.

Better Sex

How to exercise your love muscle and have better sex. The Kegel exercise, which strengthens the pubococcygeal muscle—the muscle responsible for controlling urination—can enhance your love life. *Reason:* It can prevent premature ejaculation in men and allow them to make love longer...and help women experience better orgasms. *How to perform the exercise:* For 10 minutes each morning and evening, contract this muscle as if you were holding back the flow of urine. Do 36 contractions at a time and rest a couple of minutes before beginning again. For best results, practice this exercise for several weeks.

Source: Dr. Domeena Renshaw, Loyola University Medical School, Chicago.

The Easy Cures for Male Infertility

•Male fertility problems result from inferior production, quality, and movement of sperm. Some factors to take into account…

•Age. Sperm production drops sharply after age 30.

•Alcohol. Too much lowers the production of the male hormone testosterone.

•Caffeine. Coffee and medications with caffeine appear to make sperm sluggish.

•Cimetidine. Prescribed to treat ulcers, it decreases testosterone levels.

•Clothing. Tight trousers or underwear can overheat sperm-producing cells in testicles, which lowers sperm count.

•Diethylstilbestrol. A drug used during the 1950s to prevent miscarriage, it has been found to cause fertility trouble in men whose mothers used it.

•Hot tubs. Frequent use can lower sperm count by overheating sperm-producing cells.

•Infection. All sexually transmitted diseases can have an adverse effect on fertility.

•A partner's vaginal douches, lubricants, and sprays can immobilize sperm.

•Recreational drugs. Marijuana and other drugs may decrease testosterone levels.

•Smoking. Lowers sperm count and slows sperm mobility.

Source: A Doctor's Guide to Men's Private Parts by James H. Gilbaugh, Jr., MD. Copyright 1989 by James H. Gilbaugh, Jr., MD. Reprinted by permission of Crown Publishers, 201 E. 50 St., New York 10022.

Safer Sex for Heart Patients

Location: A familiar, quiet setting. A strange environment can add to stress. *Time:* When rested and relaxed—perhaps in the morning or during the day, after a nap. Eat one to three hours before so digestion is complete. Take medications—nitroglycerin, etc.—beforehand to prevent chest pain. *Positions:* Whatever is most comfortable and familiar—it's not usually necessary to change these habits to decrease possible strain on the heart. *Helpful:* Foreplay. It gradually prepares the heart for the increased activity of intercourse.

Source: Medical Aspects of Human Sexuality, 500 Plaza Dr., Secaucus, NJ 07094.

The Prostate Gland Can Be A Blessing or a Burden

When it's working properly, the prostate gland contributes to a man's sexual pleasure. But when dysfunction occurs, it not only hinders a man's sex life but can cause other kinds of distress as well.

What are the usual things that go wrong with the prostate?

Among young men—aged 20 to 40—we see a lot of prostatitis, an inflammation of the gland. The condition produces a wide range of symptoms…sexual dysfunction (including premature ejaculation and impotence), discomfort in the lower abdomen or genital area, and difficulty in urination (such as a frequent and urgent need to urinate). In most cases, the disease is caused by a virus or bacteria and requires treatment by a physician.

Variation: Prostatosis, a congestion of the gland, which is less serious than prostatitis. It's not usually caused by an infection. But doctors aren't sure what causes it.

Are there home remedies for alleviating the distress?

Fortunately, prostatosis sometimes responds to home treatments…warm baths of 10 to 15 minutes twice a day, drinking plenty of fluids, staying away from spicy foods and alcohol. But there's not much you can do at home to treat prostatitis. As we learn more about prostate diseases, we're finding that some of the treatments we thought were effective really do nothing.

What about prostate massage? Many men claim it brings relief.

We used to think it was important, but now we realize that increased sexual activity is just as good…and more pleasurable.

Is there any connection between frequency of ejaculation and problems with the prostate?

We think not. The illness is too vague to make any connection obvious.

What about sexual activity?

It depends on the patient. If problems develop during a period of frequent sexual activity, we advise him to cut back. But if an attack occurs during a lull in activity, we suggest more frequency. It often helps. We also know that sometimes the episode has an emotional component. But, frankly, we're not sure whether the attack causes the emotional reaction or the emotions cause the attack.

What about enlarged prostates?

That disease is fairly common among older men, 60 and up. *What happens:* Since urine flows through the hole in the doughnut-shaped prostate, when the gland becomes enlarged and the hole is made smaller, the patient has trouble urinating. The only medical treatment is surgery...removal of the part of the gland that's enlarged, not all of it.

How does removal of part of the gland affect sexuality?

There's no negative effect on overall health. Usually a man can still get an erection and ejaculate—but instead of ejaculating through the penis, the semen sometimes falls back into the bladder—retrograde ejaculation.

Can the patient still father a child?

If he's intent on it, yes. It's possible to collect the semen from the urine and impregnate his wife by artificial insemination.

And cancer of the prostate?

Again, there's no way to prevent it. Once it occurs, treatment is either surgery to remove the entire gland or radiation if it hasn't spread.

Source: E. Douglas Whitehead, MD, urologist and director of the Assn. for Male Sexual Dysfunction of New York.

AIDS Risk

Neurological exams in which the same pin for pain-receptor tests is used on more than one patient.

Source: Nurses' Drug Alert.

Oral Contraceptives and Warts

Pill users are at greater risk of getting certain sexually transmitted diseases such as chlamydia and genital warts. Chlamydia is a bacterial infection that affects the cervix, pelvic organs, and/or urethra and sometimes causes mild vaginal discharge, irritation, or burning on urination. Genital warts are painless fleshy growths caused by the human papilloma virus.

Good news: Oral contraceptives protect against severe forms of pelvic inflammatory disease (PID), an infection that causes inflammation of the uterus and/or fallopian tubes.

Source: Dr. Willard Cates, Jr., of the Centers for Disease Control's division of sexually transmitted diseases.

Gout Prevention

Having sex prevents men from getting gout. Gout is caused by high blood levels of uric acid that can crystallize to form painful deposits in joints. *New finding:* Increased sexual activity reduces uric acid levels in fertile men.

Source: Dr. T. G. C. Murrell of the University of Adelaide, Australia.

Answers to Questions About Sexuality from Middle-Aged Couples

In almost two decades as a practicing sex therapist, I have encountered nearly every sexual problem imaginable. Yet for all their differences, most couples—especially middle-aged couples—share a remarkably similar set of concerns, including passion, fidelity, and compatibility. Here are the questions I get most often, along with my answers.

My husband fears he is losing his virility. What should we do?

This is an especially common question. The problem stems not so much from the realities of aging as from the cultural fallacy that a man must be physically powerful to be a good lover. Compared with younger men, men in their 60s and older do take longer to get an erection and achieve orgasm, and their orgasms are often less intense. But these changes need not hamper a man's ability to enjoy sex and be an exciting lover. In the vast majority of cases, a middle-aged man's growing self-knowledge and life experience can more than compensate for the slight decline in his physical capacity.

Crucial: A willingness to take sex more slowly and deliberately, with less emphasis on performance and more emphasis on the pleasures of stroking and caressing. For men of any age suffering from impotence or other forms of sexual dysfunction, effective treatment is available. Some cases of impotence have specific, reversible physiological causes. These should be investigated by a urologist.

Will menopause ruin our sex life?

Many middle-aged women worry that menopause will destroy their libido and ruin sex for them and their partners. Menopause can bring about certain physiological changes—vaginal dryness or a loss of sensation, for example. Fortunately, these problems are usually treatable via the use of lubricants, estrogen replacement therapy, or homeopathic herbal remedies. Moreover, many women find that menopause actually improves their sex life. Following menopause, for instance, sex is often more spontaneous, as there is no longer any need for contraception.

Bottom line: As long as both partners are emotionally prepared for menopause, there is no physical reason for it to interfere with sexuality.

We have fallen out of sync sexually. Why?

Middle age affects men and women quite differently. Many women find middle age a time of sexual liberation. After years of relative inhibition—brought on in part by the time constraints and emotional demands of child rearing—middle-aged women begin to seek greater satisfaction from lovemaking. They have become more comfortable with their bodies, so they are more willing to experiment sexually, and they start to want more from their lovers. Unfortunately, this increasing sexuality among middle-aged women often clashes with the changing sexuality of their husbands. *Reason:* Unlike their wives, middle-aged men often find themselves becoming less, rather than more, interested in sex.

Happily, this rift can usually be repaired. *Crucial:* Honesty, communication, playfulness, tenderness, an openness to sexual experimentation and self-exploration, including masturbation. However, where there are specific sexual problems or dysfunction, sex therapy is essential. In such cases, the couple may be asked to refrain from sexual intercourse while learning once again to derive pleasure simply by touching and through foreplay. Forgoing intercourse in this manner seems strange to most couples who have been having intercourse for decades. But the payoffs in enhanced pleasure and greater intimacy are well worth the effort. For couples willing to work together with love and sensitivity, middle age can be the time during which they learn how to make love rather than merely copulate.

What's happened to my sex drive?

In some cases, a loss of libido can be traced to a crisis outside the marital bedroom: serious illness, a death in the family, the loss of a job, failure in business, increased work load, unresolved feelings of anger or resentment, etc. All can cause one or both partners to lose interest in sex. Happily, desire usually returns upon the resolution of the crisis. All that's required is a little patience.

Other cases of waning desire are more complex. For example, some people find that their libido diminishes the more intimate they become with their partner. A middle-aged man may lose interest in his wife because they know each other so intimately...and in the same way a middle-aged woman may lose interest in her husband. In such cases, the trouble usually stems from some early emotional trauma resulting in a fear of intimacy. For couples who feel this phenomenon is playing a role in their relationship, the best solution is psychotherapy.

Why doesn't my spouse turn me on anymore?

Your premise is wrong. Your spouse doesn't turn you on, nor does he/she turn you off. Each of us is responsible for turning ourselves on and off. If you are no longer aroused by your spouse's loving touch, the question to ask is, *Why am I turning myself off?* In many cases, the answer can be traced to unexpressed or unresolved feelings of anger or resentment. If you have difficulty becoming aroused, scan your mind for such feelings, then discuss them with your spouse. In other cases, a spouse unwittingly sabotages the arousal process by reviewing a mental list of his/her partner's flaws.

Better: Run a list of his/her good points. Instead of letting your thoughts wander, try focusing directly on yourself, on just how pleasurable it is to be held and caressed. Remember, the brain is your most sensitive erogenous zone.

Why do my spouse and I argue so much these days?

For most couples, middle age is the time when the kids leave home and strike out on their own. This emptying of the nest seems innocuous enough. In many cases, however, it profoundly alters the emotional dynamic that exists between a husband and wife. *Reason:* After years of concealing their sexuality and focusing on childrearing, the couple suddenly find themselves alone, with nothing and no one to keep them apart. *Typical:* Points of conflict that once were glossed over "to spare the children" flare up into big fights.

Good news: While often scary, fighting is not without its practical side. It helps couples negotiate important emotional boundaries, providing emotional "space" when necessary. A more congenial way to accomplish the same thing, however, is to learn to state your needs directly to each other, and not wait until resentment turns into a fight. If you feel grouchy, for instance, ask your mate for a couple of hours alone. That way you can create some distance without causing a fight. But remember, a little fighting is healthy.

We just don't have time for sex anymore.

Many couples who complain of not having enough time for sex are really filling their time with other activities—often so they can avoid intimacy.

And no wonder. Though they can't admit it, even to themselves, most people are terrified by true intimacy. All too many of us grow up in dysfunctional households, seeing our parents argue, suffering harsh discipline and perhaps even abuse or incest—all from the first people with whom we are close, our parents. As we grow older, we fear intimacy out of a sense of self-protection. If you really want to have sex and be intimate with your partner, you can find ways to make the time.

Source: Dagmar O'Connor, PhD, lecturer in psychiatry at Columbia University, New York City. A practicing sex therapist for two decades, Dr. O'Connor was the first Masters & Johnson–trained female sex therapist in New York City. She is the author of *How to Make Love to the Same Person for the Rest of Your Life—and Still Love It* and *How to Put the Love Back into Making Love*, Bantam Doubleday Dell, 666 Fifth Ave., New York 10103.

The Secret to a Lasting Marriage

Lasting marriages owe less to true love, great sex, or even a sense of commitment than to an intimate friendship between husband and wife. In a survey, 351 couples married 15 years or longer were asked how their marriages survived in an increasingly turbulent world. Most respondents credited a positive attitude toward their spouses, as characterized by such statements as "My spouse is my best friend", and "I like my spouse as a person." Though such sentiments sound trite, they truly spell the difference between a union that lasts and one that ends in divorce.

Source: Robert Lauer, PhD, professor of human behavior, US International University, San Diego.

Easy Ways to Do Hard Things

•*Skin caught in zipper.* The best and easiest way out is to attack the zipper glide with wire clippers. At the front of the glide is a bridge that holds its top to its bottom. When you snip the bridge in two, the zipper falls apart, freeing the skin. If you try to unzip, you may pinch your skin badly.

•*Contact lenses lost in a carpet.* Place a nylon stocking over the nozzle of a vacuum cleaner and carefully vacuum the area. The lens will be pulled up onto the stocking.

•*Microwave cleaner.* Use four tablespoonfuls of baking soda to one quart of warm water. It's safer than abrasives. The same solution can be used to clean the kitchen range, too.

•*A broken water pipe can be patched* until the plumber arrives. First shut off the water. Then cut to size a piece of thick patching rubber (or use a scrap from an inner tube, doormat, or old overshoe) and wrap it around the damaged pipe. Secure the rubber with four hose clamps. You can then use the pipe temporarily with only minimal leakage.

•*Furniture scratches. For small blemishes:* Try toothpaste—its mild abrasive action is effective for minor scratches. *Deeper scratches or wide areas:* Use a blend stick, crayon, liquid shoe polish, or paste boot polish. Apply toothpaste to even out the finish after coloring. Then wax with furniture polish and buff with a clean cloth.